camaro exposed 1967–1969

Designs, Decisions and the Inside View

PAUL ZAZARINE

RB
www.
BentleyPublishers
.com

camaro exposed
1967-1969

table of contents

The basic front end came early on in the design process, see Chapter 2.

The Camaro almost lost its high cowl, see Chapter 4.

A souped up Z28, see Chapter 5.

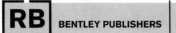

RB **BENTLEY PUBLISHERS** | Automotive Books & Manuals

Bentley Publishers, a division of Robert Bentley, Inc.
1734 Massachusetts Avenue
Cambridge, MA 02138 USA   *Information that makes*
800-423-4595 / 617-547-4170   *the difference®*
www.
BentleyPublishers
.com

Copies of this book may be purchased from selected booksellers, or directly from the publisher. The publisher encourages comments from the reader of this book. These communications have been and will be considered in the preparation of this and other books. Please write to Bentley Publishers at the address listed at the top of this page or e-mail us through our web site.

Since this page cannot legibly accomodate all the copyright notices, the Photo Credits page constitutes an extension of the copyright page.

Library of Congress Cataloging-in-Publication Data

Zazarine, Paul, 1952-
    Camaro exposed, 1967-1969 : designs, decisions, and the inside view/Paul Zazarine.
        p. cm.
    Includes index.
    ISBN 0-8376-0876-7 (pbk : alk. paper)
     1. Camaro automobile--History. I. Title.

TL215.C33 Z38 2001
629.222'2--dc21

                                                          2001035565

Bentley Stock No. GCH9
05 04 03 02 01   10 9 8 7 6 5 4 3 2 1

The paper used in this publication is acid free and meets the requirements of the National Standard for Information Sciences-Permanence of Paper for Printed Library Materials. (∞)

Camaro Exposed: 1967–1969: Designs, Decisions and the Inside View, by Paul Zazarine

Manufactured in the United States of America

Front Cover: *Z/28 in Bolero Red in base trim package and front bumper guards.* Photograph courtesy Paul Zazarine

Back Cover Photographs: Top: *Powered by a 396 engine, Camaro paced the 51st Indianapolis 500 on May 30 1967.* Photo courtesy IMS; Middle: *Yenko Camaros are distinguished by their custom interiors an exterior graphics.* Photo courtesy Paul Zazarine; Bottom: 1969 *Daytona Yellow RS/SS.* Photo courtesy Paul Zazarine.

introduction

It seems appropriate that a book about the first-generation Camaro would be published just as the fourth generation of Chevrolet's pony-car faces extinction. As in 1972, sales of the Camaro and Firebird have fallen far below expectations. But unlike in 1972 when the impassioned pleas of Chevrolet's Alex Mair and Pontiac's Bill Collins saved the F-car, in today's General Motors the decision to kill the cars will be made by accountants who—as A. J. Foyt once observed—don't know one end of a spark plug from another.

The term ponycar isn't in the new car lexicon anymore; it's part of a different era in American automotive history. It represents a time when performance meant more than fuel economy and conquest meant taking sales away from Ford and Chrysler, not Nissan and Toyota. In many respects, the Camaro has grown up; it's more refined then ever before, and, when equipped with the awesome LS1 engine, it rivals big brother Corvette in handling and acceleration. But that is the present. This book is dedicated to the past.

This is a celebration of how Detroit did business four decades ago. It recounts how the most powerful car company in the world underestimated the potential of a market tapped by arch-rival Ford and then came roaring back with a superb product that has become the stuff of legends. The Camaro was the consummate street machine of the late sixties and early seventies. From the screaming small block Z/28 to the ground-pounding SS396 and the ultimate COPO 427s, the Camaro could hold its own against virtually any car on the street, strip, or road course.

This book also celebrates the many people who worked long and hard to make the Camaro a success. To name all those who had a hand in the development of the 1967–1969 Camaro would not be possible.

To focus on the band of individuals who nurtured the Camaro—and especially the Z/28—would not be entirely equitable; they will be the first to tell you it was a team effort, both inside and outside of Chevrolet Motor Division. Suffice to say, some of the best and brightest were there for the conception and birth of the Camaro's first generation, and many of them went on to build a host of other great cars for GM.

Although this book tells the story of the original Camaro, it also reflects the heritage of today's Camaro, because the car remains true to its original matrix after 35 years. Then, as now, the Camaro was a statement about GM's ability to compete and win in the automotive marketplace. Of course, part of that success was due to GM's 50 percent dominance of the market, a presence they will never enjoy again. The automotive industry has changed dramatically in the last three decades, and GM top management failed to change with it. Fortunately for GM, its middle management never lost cognition of what the corporation stood for as it went through decades of spasmodic reiterations that have yet to end.

I am proud to dedicate this book to those men and women of Chevrolet Motor Division and GM who, then as now, are committed to building the best cars in the world.

Paul Zazarine
Florida, 2001

The 1960 Corvair Monza Club Coupe launched the sporty car concept that included bucket seats.

Chapter One
GM Sleeps as Ford Reaps

In the late fifties, a backlash began to grow against the chrome-laden behemoths being produced by Detroit. The excess in size and ornamentation turned many buyers off. They began to look for alternatives that more suited their taste and pocketbooks.

American consumers turned to imported cars such as Volkswagen, Renault, and a variety of English makes such as Austin, MG, and Rover. These cars were smaller in size, more economical to operate, and, for some owners, made a definite anti-Detroit statement. Aside from Volkswagen products, most of the other makes were unreliable and required constant maintenance, unlike most American cars. The woes of Renault and the English brands, along with their thin string of parts and service support, assured these makes would fail in the American market by the mid-to-late-sixties.

Only one American carmaker—Rambler—took immediate notice of this small car trend and began aggressively marketing their products in the compact and economy car classes. Rambler President George Romney was adamantly against big cars and sung the virtues of compacts. In 1959, Rambler rode the crest of the compact car wave by capturing 374,240 new buyers. The following year, Rambler sales pegged at 458,841, earning them the coveted third place in sales behind perennial leaders Chevrolet and Ford.

Although overall sales of imports and Rambler products remained a small percentage of the total market, The Big Three reacted by fielding their own compact cars in 1960–1961. Chrysler introduced the Valiant in 1960, and General Motors released a slew of compacts from every

American Compact Car Sales

Rambler
| | |
1959   374,240

1960   458,841

Plymouth Valiant
1960   194,292*

Dodge Lancer
1961   74,773*

Ford Falcon
1960   435,676*

Mercury Comet
1960   116,331*

Buick Special
1961   86,858*

Oldsmobile F85
1961   69,609*

Pontiac Tempest
1961   107,783*

Chevrolet Corvair
1960   250,007*

* First-year production

division except Cadillac in 1961. Chevrolet's entry into the compact market came in 1960 with an unusual air-cooled, horizontally opposed rear engine model named the Corvair that featured independent rear suspension. Ford built a miniaturized version of the big Ford and dubbed it the Falcon. To Ford chief Robert McNamera, the no-nonsense, low-cost Falcon would appeal to cost-conscious consumers. He was right. First-year production topped out at 435,676 units compared to Corvair sales of 250,007.

In February 1960, at the Chicago Auto Show, Chevrolet introduced a new Corvair model, the Monza. Basically a dolled-up 700 series, the

Edward N. Cole conceived the idea of the Corvair in 1956, the year he was appointed as General Manager for Chevrolet. Cole, who had been the Division's Chief Engineer, was a firm believer in the Corvair's air-cooled rear engine and its independent rear suspension.

Monza featured a sunroof and, more importantly, bucket seats. The response was overwhelming, and Chevrolet released the Monza for sale in April 1960. Within two years, sales of the sporty Monza had outstripped all other Corvair models. Total production for 1962 was 306,023 units, of which 216,400 were Monzas. Bucket seats accounted for over 64 percent of Monza sales. With its sporty looks and optional 150-horsepower turbocharged engine, the Monza was defining the American sporty car market.

To compete with the Monza, Ford dressed up the 1962 Falcon with the optional Futura Sprint series that featured bucket seats, upgraded interior and exterior trim, wire wheel covers, and a 260-cube V8 engine. The market responded to the Futura, buying 27,331 units in 1963. The Monza continued to own the personal sporty car market, selling 204,829 copies, of which 80 percent were equipped with bucket seats and 44 percent had four-speed manual gearboxes. The optional Spyder package included special trim and the 150-horsepower turbocharged engine with special, heavy-duty internal componentry.

It was in 1964 that the market began to diverge. The compacts were turning into midsize models, leaving the Falcon and Corvair to compete head to head. Their sporty manner, high fun-to-drive quotient, and low price made them attractive to young buyers. Demographic studies commissioned by Detroit indicated that the first wave of Baby Boomers born after the Second World War would soon be ready to purchase their first car, and all indications were that they would respond to a sporty car that provided good performance and had a back seat for gro-

Monza Spyder earned the
title of "Poor Man's Porsche"
with turbocharged engine,
independent rear suspension,
bucket seats, and four-speed
manual gearbox.

The Corvair's rear engine
was air-cooled and with turbocharger produced 150
horsepower, plenty of scoot to
motivate a car that weighed
2500 pounds.

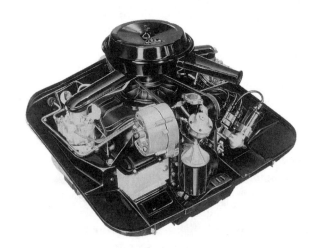

ceries and the kids. Whoever got to market first with a car with this appeal would strike gold.

Lee Iacocca already had that vision. In the early sixties, Ford's *wunderkind* executive foresaw an emerging market of youthful buyers who would be attracted to a new kind of personal car priced within their reach. This new car, which would have some of the traits of the Thunderbird but at a lower price, would be styled to appeal to young tastes, have a sporty bucket seat interior, and bear a name that suggested speed and agility. It would be cheap to build by basing it on the Falcon platform and using much of the Falcon's componentry. All that was necessary to bring this new car to market was new sheet metal and a restyled interior.

Iacocca's new car was called the Mustang. Not only did it literally toss the automotive industry on its collective ear, the Mustang instantly

Ford's answer to the Corvair Monza was the Falcon Futura. It was offered with either six or eight cylinders, which exposed the Corvair's greatest flaw – it couldn't be equipped with a V8.

captured the heart and soul of America. Introduced on April 17, 1964, at the 1964 World's Fair in New York, the Mustang was also displayed to the public at special showings across the country. Dealers were swamped with orders (26,000 on the first day). The accolades poured in, including the Tiffany Award for Excellence in American Design (the first time an automobile had ever won the coveted award from America's foremost jeweler) and appearances on the covers of both *Time* and *Newsweek*. Iacocca's vision of a car that America could fall in love with was dead on

It seemed that the Monza had captured the hearts of sporty car enthusiasts by 1963, selling over 204,000 units. The future seemed bright for the Corvair, with a magnificent rear-engined show car named it after it, the Monza GT.

The first Mustang show car gave no indications of what was truly to come. This two-seater seemed geared more toward the Corvette at the time.

target. The Mustang sold like no new car had ever sold before—over 121,000 in its short (four months) first-model year and then over a half million in 1965. Within 24 months, over one million Mustangs had been sold. The River Rouge assembly plant couldn't build them fast enough, forcing Ford to convert two additional plants to produce enough Mustangs to meet the overwhelming demand.

For GM, the introduction of the Mustang came as no surprise. The word had been out for some time that Ford was about to launch a variation of the Falcon. The automotive press had been running stories, renderings, and spy shots for several seasons, conjecturing about the new Ford entry. What torpedoed GM was its failure to anticipate just what Ford was about to unveil, its underestimation of the new model's impact on the emerging Youth Market and its inability to be ready with a competitive model.

There are several reasons why GM slept while Ford cleaned up at the showrooms, and most of them had to do with overconfidence and arrogance. Although a short wheelbase, personal sporty car had been done in clay and presented for consideration, GM management didn't feel it was necessary to add an additional model to the Chevrolet line-up. With the big Chevy, Corvette, Chevy II, Corvair, and the new-for-1964 Chevelle, management believed all the bases were covered and there was no niche the upcoming Ford could carve that didn't already have a Bow Tie on it. As far as the sporty car market was concerned, the Corvette covered the high end and the Corvair Monza the low end. The Monza had been a successful seller with its bucket seats, sporty styling, and peppy six-cylinder air-cooled, rear-mounted engine. GM management believed there was no way the new Ford could go head to head with the Monza Spyder. With 1963 sales of 254,000 units

The Mustang II show-car was the harbinger of things to come. Other than windshield rake, bumpers and other minor details, the Mustang II was close to production specs.

Above: The Mustang was released in April 1964 and was an instant hit. General Motors failed to realize the huge new market Ford had tapped.

Right: The Corvair was restyled for 1965 and featured new design themes that would echo through other GM cars through the rest of the decade. The sleek lines, rounded body shape and kicked up quarterpanels were fresh ideas. GM management firmly believed the new Corvair could go head to head against the Mustang.

(204,000 of which were Monzas), the Corvair owned the low-price sporty car market.

What crippled the Corvair was it only offered a rear-positioned, horizontally opposed air-cooled six-cylinder engine, while the Mustang, with its conventional drivetrain configuration, offered six-cylinder or V8 power. Consequently, the Mustang appealed to a market that was enamored by the V8. By ignoring the voice of the consumer, GM's arrogance cost the corporation millions of dollars. It was this disdain for the customer's desires that would be GM's downfall.

As soon as the Mustang hit the streets, GM knew it was in trouble. The Corvair felt the impact of the Mustang's presence almost immediately. Corvair sales for 1964 tumbled (the Monza suffered a decline of over 63,000 units), and even a fresh restyle in 1965 could do little to halt the Mustang juggernaut. By 1966, total Corvair sales had dropped to just over 100,000 units. The final nail in the Corvair's coffin was an article that appeared in *The Nation*, written by a young lawyer named Ralph Nader, who claimed the Corvair's swing rear axle design was dangerous and responsible for hundreds of accidents and tens of deaths. Nader expanded the thesis into a best-selling book called *Unsafe at Any Speed*, an expose of the early Corvair's oft-time bizarre rear suspension characteristics. It didn't take long before the media had picked up on the story, and although the Corvair's handling peccadilloes had been corrected, the car's credibility was destroyed.

Internally, GM was aware that the early Corvair's independent suspension could cause accidents. The severe camber change when the rear was unloaded would cause the wheels to tuck under, creating an adhesion and handling problem. While a professional test driver on a closed course was capable of driving through the problem, an average driver on the street had his hands full, and the possibility of losing con-

By the beginning of the 1965 model year, Ford had sold over 100,000 Mustangs and GM was waking to the news that they had missed the boat.

trol was real. In fact, Chevrolet General Manager Bunkie Knudsen's niece experienced an accident in a Corvair that was traced to the unusual characteristics of the independent rear suspension

By the spring of 1966, over one hundred lawsuits had been filed against the early Corvairs, and the negative press and congressional investigations had destroyed the car's image as well as its marketing potential and resale value. Any chance the Corvair could hold off the Mustang until GM could pony up a competitor withered as the heat of the controversy continued to rise. In April 1964, GM management finally felt the competitive pressure to build a ponycar-class car after Mustang production hit 100,000 units. By then, Ford's substantial lead in sales and momentum was so tremendous it would carry sales for several more years.

As for the Corvair, sales plummeted as customers stayed away in droves. The automotive press praised the redesigned and restyled Corvair for its good looks, excellent handling, and positive performance. Unfortunately, the die was cast, and by 1967, the Corvair was an afterthought in the Chevrolet product lineup, selling only 27,253 base Corvair 500s and Monzas. Production of Corvairs was halted in April 1969 after only 6,000 units had been sold. Since the Corvair's resale value had been so badly damaged, Chevrolet offered buyers of 1969 Corvairs a $150 discount coupon good through 1973 that they could

Making the Corvair Illegal

Just as Ralph Nader was becoming a household name and the Corvair was unfairly earning a reputation as an unsafe car, the Michigan legislature tried to legislate it and other rear-engined cars off the road.

Filed in 1966, Michigan Senate Bill 773 sought to ban from state roads 1960–1963 Corvairs, Volkswagens, Porsches, Renaults, and other rear-engined cars. The bill was placed in the legislature after two jury trials against GM, one in Florida and the other in California, had been dismissed. The media has sensationalized the two trials, and although in each the Corvair's swing rear axle was exonerated, it was intimated that the car was essentially a killer. In response, the Michigan bill called for standards of lateral acceleration that most cars built at the time, not only rear-engined models, could not meet.

The bill eventually died in the legislature; however, it indicated the growing concern among lawmakers and automotive critics about the Corvair and its swing rear axle. Three years after Michigan Senate Bill 773, the Corvair was quietly discontinued.

use to buy any new Chevrolet product. It was an embarrassing admission on GM's part that the Corvair couldn't hold its value in the used car market.

As the Corvair faded into obscurity at the end of the decade, Chevrolet was already deep in the throes of the ponycar wars, its weapon being the Camaro. Few cared to remember that only seven years before the Corvair had been America's popular sporty car, introducing bucket seats to the mainstream market, selling hundreds of thousands of cars, and setting standards that would be reflected in its successor, the 1967 Camaro.

Chevrolet General Manager Elliot "Pete" Estes stands in front of a gleaming
Bolero Red Rally Sport. Estes was the unsung hero who, behind the scenes, sup-
ported many great GM musclecars like the GTO and the Z/28.

Chapter Two
1967—The Rush to Market

The origins of the Camaro can be traced to the first week of April 1964, when vehicle number 64163 was tested at the General Motors Proving Grounds. That vehicle was a 1964 1/2 Mustang hardtop with a six-cylinder engine and three-speed manual transmission. A copy of the 2,000-mile break-in test report, dated April 6, 1964, indicates GM had already procured and was testing a new Mustang 11 days prior to the public introduction of Ford's new ponycar. According to Alex Mair, who joined the Camaro platform in 1966 as Chief Passenger Car Engineer, GM and Ford had a reciprocity agreement in those days to supply each other with new products for analysis prior to introduction. "We always had Ford products 2–4 weeks ahead of the formal announcement. It was a shake-hands agreement that the public didn't know about."

Although it would take four months before GM management gave the go-ahead to start on the F-car (F was the corporation's designation for the new body), Chevrolet Engineering was already at work targeting the Mustang's basic specifications and dimensions for their ponycar. Stylists used the 1964 Super Nova show car as a starting point for the F-car, also designated Project XP-836.

When work began on the F-car in August 1964, a set of specific baselines were established by Chevrolet for the final design:

- Distinctively modern aerodynamic styling for a clean functional appearance
- Small, highly maneuverable size with packaging for four passengers

- A very broad range of available performance capability
- Quick, sharply defined roadability with a firm, yet comfortable ride
- "Cockpit-type" interiors for close driver identification
- An evolutionary, rather than revolutionary, basic design approach to maintain maximum value to the customer
- Wide selection of mechanical and appearance equipment to allow customer tailoring to his needs and desires

Test sheet from GM's Milford Proving Grounds documenting road test of the 1964 Mustang, dated April 6, 1964, 11 days prior to the Mustang's introduction.

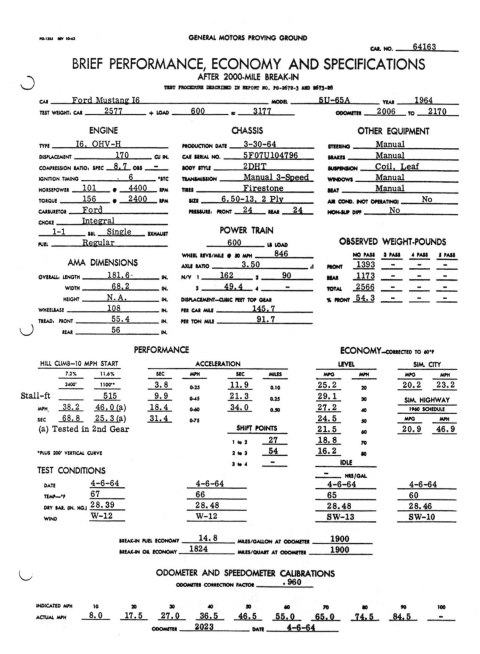

Chevrolet Engineering broke down the design and construction of the Camaro with four major construction groups:

- Bolted-on front-end sheet metal
- Unitized body construction with the rear framing elements incorporated into the underbody
- Driveline, solid driving rear axle and single leaf rear suspension combined into a simple and efficient Hotchkiss drive system
- A front chassis unit consisting of the engine, transmission, front suspension, front brakes, and steering gear and linkage mounted on a separate, extended rail partial front frame.

Chassis Engineer Paul King recalled the pressure involved as the original perimeters of the F-car were laid out. "I was in the development group at the time," King remembers. "We were getting a lot of stuff pumped into the car from other directions than usual. Road noise and road impact were harder to isolate. If there was an assembly consideration, we had the manufacturing people on our side. They were concerned about line spacing on the assembly line, so the overall length of the vehicle was important. We were pressured to get a car like the Mustang out both in image and in price. That forced us to want to do the car in a big hurry."

To reduce engineering costs, part of the F-car's structural design was shared with the 1968 Chevy II. Since its introduction in 1962, the Chevy II had utilized unit body construction, to which all chassis components were attached to framing elements incorporated into the underbody. Ford had used this same type of construction on the

The Camaro's body was unitized construction. The doors and deck lid were double panel steel construction.

Although the Camaro was a unitized car, the front end was assembled like a composite body/frame car. That allowed the Camaro to be built on the same assembly line as other Chevrolet products.

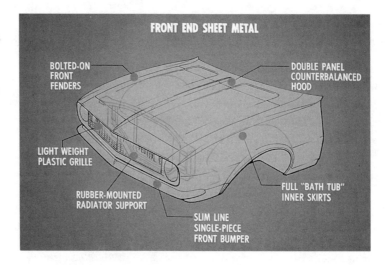

FRONT END SHEET METAL

BOLTED-ON FRONT FENDERS

DOUBLE PANEL COUNTERBALANCED HOOD

LIGHT WEIGHT PLASTIC GRILLE

RUBBER-MOUNTED RADIATOR SUPPORT

FULL "BATH TUB" INNER SKIRTS

SLIM LINE SINGLE-PIECE FRONT BUMPER

The body/frame integral design was strengthened construction and boxed roof rails.

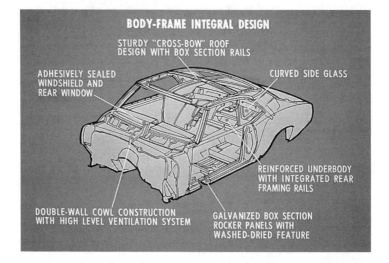

BODY-FRAME INTEGRAL DESIGN

STURDY "CROSS-BOW" ROOF DESIGN WITH BOX SECTION RAILS

ADHESIVELY SEALED WINDSHIELD AND REAR WINDOW

CURVED SIDE GLASS

REINFORCED UNDERBODY WITH INTEGRATED REAR FRAMING RAILS

DOUBLE-WALL COWL CONSTRUCTION WITH HIGH LEVEL VENTILATION SYSTEM

GALVANIZED BOX SECTION ROCKER PANELS WITH WASHED-DRIED FEATURE

The Camaro was the first GM vehicle to feature a separate subframe that the front suspension bolted to and cradled the engine. The subframe connected to the body at four attaching points, two beneath the cowl and two located under the front seats. By doing so, engine and road noise were reduced while handling was improved.

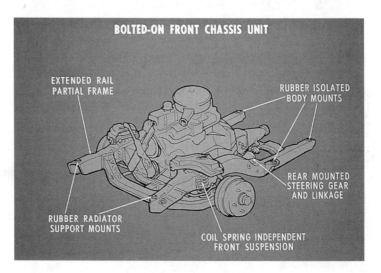

BOLTED-ON FRONT CHASSIS UNIT

EXTENDED RAIL PARTIAL FRAME

RUBBER ISOLATED BODY MOUNTS

REAR MOUNTED STEERING GEAR AND LINKAGE

RUBBER RADIATOR SUPPORT MOUNTS

COIL SPRING INDEPENDENT FRONT SUSPENSION

Falcon. It was an inexpensive way to build a low-price car; however, it left much to be desired since the cars were prone to creaks, rattles, and harsh rides. Using a full frame beneath the F-car would have been too costly, so GM engineers borrowed from several European designs. They adapted an extended-rail front subframe that would attach to a unit body using four rubber body bushings—two at the cowl dash legs and two in the area under the front seats where the subframe ended. The use of rubber body bushings isolated the passenger compartment from vibrations, road noise, and engine noise. The transmission was attached to a crossmember at the rear of the subframe. At the front of the subframe were two additional mounts for front sheet metal attachment, similar to composite body/full frame Chevrolet cars like the Chevelle.

Using the 1965 Corvair as a target, Chevrolet engineers chose to make the F-car lower in height with a more pronounced long hood/short deck look while still incorporating some of the Corvair's "coke-bottle" kick-up of the leading edge of the rear quarters. By assigning the F-car a wheelbase of 108 inches, the front overhang measured in at 36.6 inches and left a relatively short rear deck. This proportioning allowed the instrument panel, cowl, and front seats to be positioned more to the rear, comparable to the Corvette rather than the Chevy II. Stylists would still have to struggle with the high cowl that was inherited by this shared design, and several different approaches to cowl height and hood length would be attempted.

By combining a subframe attached to a unit body, Chevrolet Engineering was able to achieve several cost savings. The subframe was designed to accept the standard GM design SLA front suspension with

Because the Camaro and the Chevy II shared the same subframe, they also shared the same cowl height and steering wheel angle. This wooden buck was built to the Camaro's basic engineering dimensions. From there designers began their work on styling the Camaro's body.

With a wheelbase of 108 inches and moderate over-hang front and rear, the Camaro had the long hood, short deck theme essential for a pony car. The high cowl and steering column from the upcoming 1968 Chevy II irritated designers and stylists.

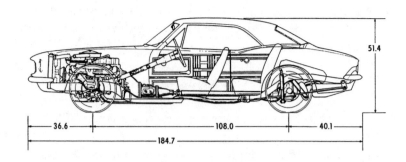

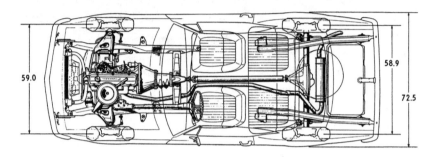

INTERIOR DIMENSIONS
Sport Coupe (Inches)

Head Room, Effective	Front	37.7
	Rear	36.5
Leg Room, Effective	Front	42.5
	Rear	29.9
Shoulder Room	Front	56.7
	Rear	53.8
Entrance Height		29.3
Luggage Capacity	Total	19.6
(Cubic Feet)	Usable	8.3

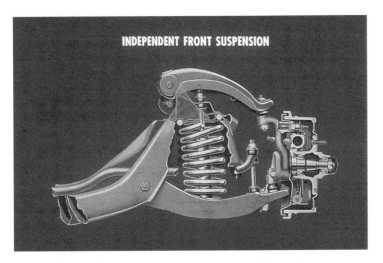

The Camaro used the standard GM SLA independent suspension with Delco shocks with one-inch pistons and .6875-inch front stabilizer bar.

This was state of the art computer-aided engineering in 1965. The Camaro's body shell was mounted on a jig and then "bounced" to analyze stress and fatigue failure.

unequal length upper and lower A-arms, monotube shock, and coil spring with front stabilizer bar. The 1968 Chevy II would also significantly benefit from the F-car's developments, including the subframe, front suspension design, braking systems, and powertrains. By spreading the costing of these components across model lines, Chevrolet could keep the price per unit down, thus making the products competitive in the marketplace and still maintain a profitable margin.

As a clean-sheet project, Chevrolet Engineering applied the newest available technology in determining the characteristics of the suspension. Although primitive by today's standards, analog computer simulation techniques were used for the first time to analyze the perimeters Chevrolet engineers had designed for the F-car. The computer-simulated engineering, provided by the Engineering Mechanics Department of General Motors Research Laboratories, was essential in setting the spring deflection rates, anti-roll bar rates, shock valving, and other ride and handling characteristics.

Using computers to evaluate and analyze suspension setting was still a new science, and not everyone in Chevrolet Engineering was sold on the idea. "We were willing to gamble a little bit on some of our design decisions by what the computer told us," said Paul King. "That was a new tool for us, and we weren't sure how much confidence to put in it. You were creating a design and then making some decisions based on the computer saying 'If you do this, it will be that.' We didn't know how much credence to give to these sorts of indications. So for a while the computer analysis followed the actual design until we grew more confident of its analysis."

The rear suspension consisted of a Hotchkiss-type arrangement mounted on monoleaf semi-elliptical springs with direct, double-acting hydraulic shock absorbers. The attaching points for the rear suspension were mounted directly to reinforced points at the rear body shell. Because of the shorter length available at the rear, the chrome carbon steel leaf springs were 6.5 inches shorter than the Chevy II's 62.5-inch springs and 2.5 pounds lighter. To deliver excellent handling characteristics but still provide adequate body isolation, a computer program was devised to analyze suspension reaction to changes in bushing durometer. The tests revealed that a single, low-durometer bushing was ideal for the front spring bushing, and, at the rear, two-piece bushings from lower durometer rubber were utilized. This combination provided the sought-after compromise between rear suspension control and body isolation from drivetrain and road noise.

Computer analyses also revealed that the rear shock absorbers should be mounted outboard of the springs in an almost vertical arrangement as opposed to the standard diagonal configuration. Chevrolet engineers determined that this would improve tire adhesion on washboard road surfaces and improve cornering. Engineer Paul King remembers that it was only later that they discovered that the springs wound up under severe braking or severe launch. It was worse with the big block cars, which generated tremendous torque on the rear suspension assembly. Several methods to eliminate the problem were explored, including frame ties that would have tied the trailing edge of the front subframe to the leading edge of the rear spring. Cost considerations shot that idea down, and the basic design format was retained

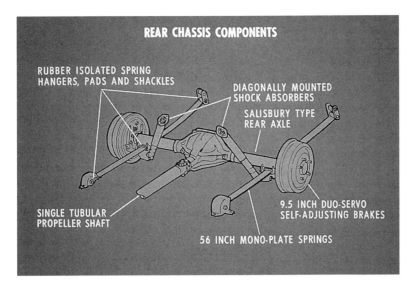

REAR CHASSIS COMPONENTS

RUBBER ISOLATED SPRING
HANGERS, PADS AND SHACKLES

DIAGONALLY MOUNTED
SHOCK ABSORBERS

SALISBURY TYPE
REAR AXLE

SINGLE TUBULAR
PROPELLER SHAFT

9.5 INCH DUO-SERVO
SELF-ADJUSTING BRAKES

56 INCH MONO-PLATE SPRINGS

The Mono-Plate rear springs were prone to wind up and axle tramp. Among the many fixes suggested was to tie the rear of the front subframe to the front of the rear spring mount. That was too costly and the concept abandoned.

until the end of the 1967 model year. However, a traction bar was added to the right monospring, which cured some of the wheelhop problems.

Preproduction mules (disguised in Chevy II sheet metal), as well as a group of competitor cars, were driven across the United States from New England to California and to GM's Desert Proving Grounds near Phoenix in September 1964. Several were also taken to GM's Milford, Michigan, Proving Grounds to demonstrate the difference between the computer simulations, which were constrained by the design perimeters, and real-world test conditions. The first pretest vehicle provided directional control response baseline measurements that were then compared to the computer data. The results indicated that the real-world characteristics of the suspension design were in line with the low lateral acceleration computer simulations. The contrary was true at high lateral acceleration, with the mule having more understeer. Roll rates and angles were 10 percent lower, indicating the suspension did not share the simulation's characteristics.

When the engineering specifications for the new F-car arrived on designer Henry Haga's desk in Chevrolet's Studio II on August 26, it was obvious that there was a lot of Chevy II architecture in the numbers. These specifications required the same numbers for the height of the cowl and the distance from the center of the front axle to the dash as did the Chevy II specifications. For the bread and butter Chevy II, these numbers would proportion nicely into a two- or four-door design. For the F-car, however, it resulted in a cowl that was too high in the eye of the designers and not enough distance from the

Going West

Any engineer worth his slide rule will tell you that when you chop the top off a body, you lessen structural rigidity and induce body shake over rough and uneven road surfaces. To compensate for this torsional "twist," chassis braces are usually installed to shore up the body flexing.

That's what happened to the 1967 Camaro convertible. As Alex Mair remembers, "Pete Estes [Chevrolet General Manager] drove the convertible and it shook like a 1940 Buick four-door convertible. It was bad, even though it was an integral car. Pete ordered engineering to 'fix that!'"

"Pete used to have a saying," Mair said, "and he was such a great guy to work for—he'd ask you to do something and if it wasn't done, he'd say 'Listen young man, if you don't get that done, you go West until your hat floats.'"

Charlie Rubly worked on the shake and tried everything he could think of to engineer it out. As Paul King recalls, "The entire car shook. Our last resort was to use seismic dampers, which were expensive and heavy and an embarrassment." Rubly installed the dampers, called 'cocktail shakers,' in the trunk and front engine compartment. The modification made an immediate difference. Estes took another ride and was pleased with the results until he found out the "fix" would cost $50 per car. "I've finally found out when to send you West to float your hat," Estes announced to Mair. Costly as they were, the cocktail shakers were engineered into every 1967–1969 F-car convertible.

Located in the trunk and front end of convertible models, these "cocktail shakers" were seismic dampers that reduced torsional body twist and shake. That twist resulted from removing the roof and with it, the integrity it contributed to the body's overall rigidity.

front wheel to the dash. Designers worked to get a lower look to the cowl by giving the windshield a more severe rake and by thinning the A pillars.

By December 1964, the basic shell was completed. The look was fluid, a new approach in GM that had started with the 1965 Corvair and appeared on many restyled 1966 GM cars. Angles and beveled lines were smoothed into flowing curves, with quarter panels ramping upwards (the famous GM "Coke bottle" look) and integrating the C-pillar from top to deck. From the front, the body had a fuselage appearance as it rolled down into the rocker panels. The curved side glass area

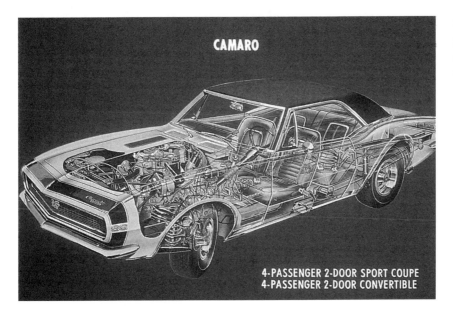

Cutaway view of the Camaro package reveals high cowl architecture inherited from the 1968 Chevy II design.

By mid-January 1965, the Camaro's shape and styling was in place. Even this early in the process, the basic headlamp, grille, and thin bladed bumper design were already in place.

Right: The high quarter panel kickup (also known as the "Coke bottle") is clearly established here, however the tail lamps and rear panel had not yet been resolved.

Below: One month later, proposals for window moldings, quarter window trim, feature lines, and wheel cutouts, and tail lamps were being studied.

This scale model of the Camaro was taken to the wind tunnel to test the car's aerodynamics. By using ink stains, engineers could determine airflow over and around the vehicle. Remarkably, the Camaro required little modification based on the extensive tests made in the wind tunnel.

and flowing rear deck strongly contradicted the Mustang's chiseled look, and although the dimensions of the two ponycars were virtually identical, the F-car's design was more fluid and streamlined. Chevrolet highlighted the curved contours of the F-car's design and noted "one interesting styling aspect of these rounded beauty surfaces is the feeling of motion achieved by light reflections while the car is stationary as well as moving." By August 1965, the front grille, headlamp design and placement had been approved.

In fact, when taken to the wind tunnel in February 1965, the first Camaro quarter-scale models exhibited excellent aerodynamic characteristics. In attendance were a Chevrolet engineer, a stylist, and a clay modeler. In a series of 76 tests conducted at the Voight wind tunnel in Dallas, a variety of different angles and positions were tested to accumulate data on six major forces affecting aerodynamics: Lift, drag, side forces, pitching, yawing, and rolling moments were all recorded and fed into a computer. Airflow visualization tests using the ink stain method were also performed and photographed after each test was run. The end result of this 11-day testing showed the basic design of the F-car to be remarkably smooth and requiring very little tweaking. Styling cleaned up the leading edges of the front fenders and reduced the front valance rake. Some of the testing done at this time was utilized for the Z/28's chin and rear spoiler.

In retrospect, it was fortunate that the Camaro's body proved to be inherently aerodynamic since there wasn't adequate time in the schedule to experiment with radically different designs and still deliver the car to market in the fall of 1966. Engineer Paul King recalls, "To me, wind tunnel testing was interesting at that time, but we were going to build the car the way it was regardless of what the wind tunnel said. We had a job to do and we were going to do it. If the wind tunnel results were positive, that was nice. If they were bad, that was too bad, because we were going to build the car anyway."

Above: Profile of Panther Rally Sport shows front header stripe with thin line extending back to rear bumper. European racing mirrors wouldn't appear until 1970 $1/2$ model. Note leaping Panther emblem on lower front fender behind wheel opening.

Right: High front view of Panther Rally Sport shows hood vents. Initially, vents were to be open to extract hot underhood air, however water drainage problems cancelled this idea. Dummy vents were used for production models. Also notice dual headlamps were to shine through grille.

This engineering mule was taken to the Milford Proving Grounds August 5, 1965 for chassis testing. The Panther nameplate is on the rear deck and license plate.

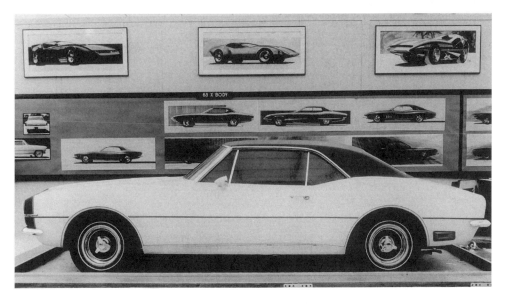

This Chaparral trim proposal has extractors located at lower rear of quarter panels. Outside rear view mirrors didn't make production, however they are very similar to exterior mirrors used on 1969 Hurst Olds.

1967 Camaro vs. 1967 Mustang
The Tale of the Tape

	Camaro	Mustang
Wheelbase (inches)	108.1	108.0
Tread (inches)		
Front	59.0	57.9
Rear	58.9	57.9
Steering		
Turns lock-to-lock		
manual/power	4.00/3.00	4.64/3.60
Turning circle (dia. ft.)	37.0	37.2
Overall length (inches)	184.6	183.6
Width (inches)	72.5	70.9
Height (inches)	51.0	51.6
Box volume (cu. ft.)	395.0	388.4
Frontal area (sq. ft.)	20.6	20.3
Hip room (inches)		
Front	56.3	53.9
Rear	54.5	50.9
Truck capacity (cu. ft.)	8.3	9.2
Fuel tank (gallons)	18.5	17.0
Brakes		
Standard	drum	drum
Optional	front disc	front disc
Brake swept area (sq. in.)	268.6	212.0
Standard tires	7.35 x 14	6.95 x 14
Curb weight (lbs.)	2900	2696
Standard engine (cid/cylinders/hp)	230/6/140	200/6/120
Optional engines (cid/cylinders/hp)	250/6/155	289/V8/200
	327/V8/210	289/V8/225
	327/V8/275	289/V8/271
	350/V8/295	390/V8/335
	396/V8/325	
Standard transmission	three-speed manual	three-speed manual
Optional transmissions	four-speed manual	four-speed manual
	two-speed automatic	three-speed automatic

This two-seat concept wears the Chaparral badge with SS front stripe. Rear overhang is awkward and proposal went no further.

Origin of "Mark" Designation on Big Blocks

This information is from a phone call from John Stier to Dick Keinath, who is now retired. Dick coined the term *Mark* for the big-block engine.

The W block series (348 and 409 cid) was produced for model years 1958–1965. In the summer of 1962, Dick Keinath started work on a replacement for the W block. It had the same bore centers (4.84 inches) as the W block. To keep things differentiated in the minds of folks working on both engines, the planned successor to the W block was dubbed Mark II. It was a big-bore, short-stroke 427 cid. It was also known as the Mystery Motor at the 1963 Daytona 500.

The W block, by definition, was the Mark I. The word *Mark* was derived from the European tradition of using *Mark* to designate succeeding phases of a design.

The Mark III was a 1963 design study that had features like the Mark II but had a bigger bore center. None were built in production. It required too much tooling money at Tonawanda to change bore centers. The Mark IV went into production in 1965 as a 396 cid. Mark IVs were subsequently produced in versions of 427 and 454 cid. Deck heights were 9.80 inches. Tall-block versions of 366 and 427 were then introduced. They had decks .4-inch taller to accommodate the fourth piston ring.

— *John Stier, Manager Mark Base Engine*

New Kid at the Drags

Chevy drag racers took to the Camaro like Bucron to asphalt. It didn't take long for racers to set up the Camaro and become competitive. While Mopar still dominated the Super Stock classes thanks to generous factory backing, the Bow Tie boys had to "shadetree" most of their buildups since GM was still "not participating" in any form of competitive racing.

Out of the chute the Camaro was right in the heat of competition. Vying for the Super Stock Eliminator title at the 1967 NHRA World Finals, 3 out of 16 qualifiers were 1967 Camaros. Leading the SS/EA pack was John Blackstock of Bay City, Michigan, with an ET of 12.12, followed by Dick Arons of Southfield, Michigan, with a 12.19 ET. In SS/C, Berwyn, Pennsylvania's Bill "Grumpy" Jenkins had turned an 11.61 ET.

At the 1967 NHRA Nationals at Indy, a 1967 Camaro won B/S with a 12.54/110.97. Dick Arons captured the SS/EA trophy with a 12.87/108.85 in his Camaro. In a fitting debut, the 1967 Camaro also captured Super Stock Eliminator (SS/C—Bill Jenkins with a 11.55/115.97) and Stock Eliminator (B/S—Ben Wenzel with a 12.33/113.92). It didn't take long for the Camaro to establish itself in the stock classes, and Chevrolet hoped this image would rub off on the street version as well. The timeworn cliché "race on Sunday and sell on Monday" was music to Chevrolet Marketing's ears.

Chevrolet had a depth and breadth of powertrains to chose from for the F-car. Since the car was to be marketed on several levels ranging from economy to high performance, a variety of engine packages were selected. Standard was the 230-cubic inch inline six-cylinder Turbo-Thrift, rated at 140 horsepower with single-barrel Rochester carburetor and mated to a three-speed all synchromesh manual gearbox located on the steering column. Standard rear axle ratio was 3.08:1. The optional two-speed automatic Powerglide was coupled to 2.73:1 rear, and the optional four-speed box came with 3.55:1 cogs standard.

The first optional engine was RPO L22 250-cubic inch inline six-cylinder Turbo-Thrift, pegged at 155 horsepower with single-barrel Rochester carburetor and using the same transmission combinations as the standard six.

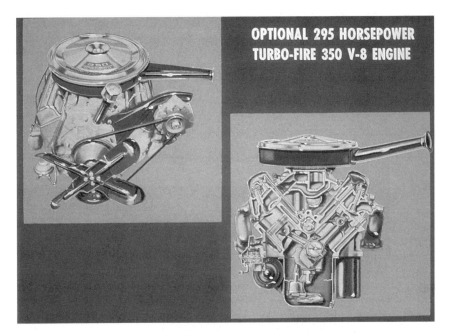

OPTIONAL 295 HORSEPOWER TURBO-FIRE 350 V-8 ENGINE

New for 1967 and exclusive to the Camaro was the 350 cubic inch small block. Rated at 295 horsepower, it was the standard engine with the SS package.

The standard L30 Turbo-FireV8 displaced 327 cubic inches and was rated at 210 horsepower with two-barrel Rochester carburetor. Standard transmission was the three-speed manual with floor mounted Inland shifter. A four-speed tranny or the two-speed Powerglide were offered as options. A second 327 was offered, this one producing 275 horsepower using a Rochester Quadra-Jet and 10.0:1 compression ratio and higher lift camshaft. It also used Chevelle-style exhaust manifolds modified to fit the F-car's chassis.

New for the Chevy powertrain lineup was the L48 Turbo-Fire 350 with 295 horsepower. This engine displacement was achieved by lengthening the crank stroke .023 inches, enlarging the crank counterweights, and lowering the piston compression height. Rochester's new Quadra-Jet four-barrel fed the 10.25:1 compression engine. Rear axle ratios ranged from a gas sipping 3.07:1 to an asphalt-melting 4.88:1. The SS package with the L48 cost an additional $210.65.

Introduced in November 1966, the top drivetrain option for the SS package was the L35 396-cubic inch Turbo-Thrust V8 that added $263.30 to the sticker price. The L35 weighed 186 pounds more than the L48, boasted 325 horsepower, and competed directly against the 390 Mustang. Components from the Corvette's 425-horse L78 engine were borrowed for the L35; however, the L35 used hydraulic lifters and smaller valve heads. The M13 heavy-duty three-speed manual gearbox was located on the floor with the L35 package. The M20 four-speed with 2.52:1 low gear and M35 two-speed Powerglide were again

1967 Performance V8 Engine Production			
RPO	CID	HP	Production
L48	350	295	29,270
L35	396	325	1,003
L78	396	375	1,138

Engine compartment is a little tight with 350 engine and air conditioning. Interestingly, this car was ordered with a/c but no power steering or power brakes.

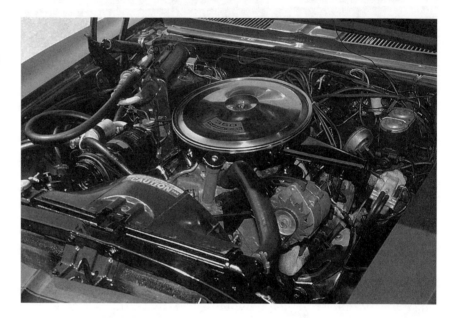

options. In midyear, Chevrolet released the much-needed M40 three-speed Turbo Hydra-Matic. Doing away with the two-speed Powerglide in favor of the Turbo Hydra-Matic made the Camaro competitive with Ford's C6 three-speed automatic.

In early 1967, Chevrolet released the L78 for use in the Camaro SS. Costing $500.30, the 375-horsepower 396 was standard with the three-speed heavy-duty duty manual gearbox, with the M20 Muncie four-speed the only optional transmission. With the four-speed, rear axle ratios were offered from 3.07:1 up to 4.88:1. The L78 featured 11.0:1 compression, solid lifters and a big Holley four-barrel with 1.562-inch primaries and secondaries. With the optional L78, the Camaro now had one of the best horsepower-to-weight ratios in the market. Amazingly, the same rear spring rates were used for the L78 (115 lbs. per in.) as the 250-cube six and the base 327 V8.

While the design and engineering of the F-car's suspension and exterior was underway, interior stylists began designing the car's

See How They Ran

Every automotive magazine road test included two fundamentals of sixties' performance—0–60 acceleration and quarter-mile performance. Here's how the Camaro ran in a variety of different powertrain combinations as tested by the automotive press.

Model	WT	Engine	HP	Trans	0–60	Quarter Mile	Magazine
2 dr. coupe	3400	250	155	3M	11.4	18.5/75	CL 3/67
2 dr. coupe	3228	327	210	PG	10.7	18.2/77	MT 12/66
SS350	3714	350	295	4M	7.8	16.1/86.5	C&D 11/66
SS396	3520	396	325	THM	6.8	15.4/92	MT 5/67

CL = Car Life   MT = Motor Trend   C&D = Car and Driver

Custom interior in black with optional console and gauge package. Notice air conditioning ducts at center top and outboard ends of panel.

interior. Working with the high Chevy II cowl and steering wheel placement relative to seating position, designers worked to pull the seating position down and rearward to give a sports-car-like feeling for the driver and front passenger.

They did so by attaching the seats directly to the floor pan, thus lowering the driver's position. The instrument panel slanted in and downward, allowing more space, and suggested lower, more intimate driving positions. The panel was covered by a foam crash pad color keyed to the interior. The gauge package was comprised of two elliptical bezels that contained the instrumentation. In the center of the panel was a matte black finished panel with bright molding containing the radio, ashtray, and horizontal sliding controls for the heater. A standard glove box was placed in the right side of the instrument panel.

Bucket seats were standard equipment on all models, however the Strato-back bench seat with fold-down center armrest was offered optionally. Vinyl seating coverings were standard as was door-to-door carpeting. The door panels were also vinyl with embossed panels and freestanding armrest.

The Custom Interior option upgraded the F-car's appearance. Color-keyed accent bands highlighted the seat cushions and seat backs on Strato-bucket seats and backseat. The door panels were molded vinyl with integral, full-length arm rests, recessed door release handles, and lower door carpeting. The steering wheel boasted chrome center spokes and color-keyed rim. The center horn button wore one of three caps: Camaro, RS, or SS depending on option packages. A steering wheel with chrome spokes and wood-grained rim was offered optionally.

Interior and Exterior Color Combinations

Interior Trim Colors

EXTERIOR	Gold	Blue	Black	Turq	Red	Brt. Blue	Parchment	Yellow
Black	•	•	•	•	•	•	•	•
White	•	•	•	•	•	•	•	•
Medium Blue		•	•			•	•	
Dark Blue		•	•			•	•	
Bright Blue		•	•			•	•	
Gold	•		•				•	•
Medium Green			•				•	
Medium Turquoise			•	•			•	
Dark Turquoise			•	•			•	
Plum			•				•	
Maroon	•		•		•		•	
Red			•		•		•	
Fawn	•		•				•	•
Cream	•		•				•	•
Yellow			•	•			•	•

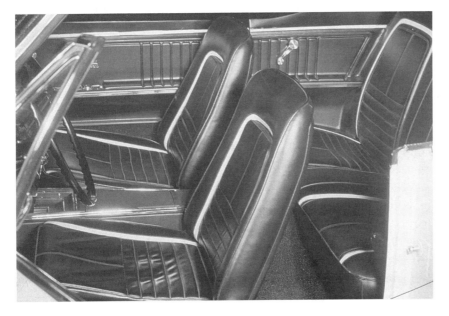

Above: The Camaro's instrument panel was well laid out with two large round pods containing gauges and telltale lamps. In the center of the panel were the HVAC controls and radio. The console was optional.

Left: Custom interior with molded door panels had integrated armrests. Contrasting inserts in seat backs and cushions broke up monochromatic look.

View of instrument panel shows optional tachometer in right hand pod and optional console-mounted gauge package. Toggle switch below ignition is not production. T-shaped shifter was standard on automatics equipped with console.

Between the bucket seats, the customer could order a custom console, which, when combined with automatic transmission, placed the shifter in the console. An optional gauge cluster consisted of fuel, temperature, oil pressure and ammeter gauges, along with a clock. Other options included fold-down rear seat, headrests, and an AM/FM stereo radio that could be combined with an 8-track stereo tape player. Air conditioning could be installed by either the factory as an integrated system or by the dealer as a hang-on package. Cruise control was a new GM option for intermediate models. Buyers could also order a remote-controlled outside rearview mirror, shoulder harnesses, and a space saver spare tire.

Chevrolet product planners chose to offer the F-car in three packages. All were based first on the Standard package, and then added other refinements and accessories. The first package was the Style Trim Group, that included front and rear wheel opening bright moldings, body side accent stripes, and bright drip gutter moldings on hardtops. The standard front end featured exposed circular headlamps, black full-width "loop" style plastic grille, and inboard-mounted parking lamps.

The optional Rally Sport package included paint stripes, bright moldings, and specific rear dual tail lamp treatment. The most notable part of the RS package was the disappearing headlamps. When concealed, lattice covers at both ends hid the headlamps. A second black grille ran the full width of the radiator grille opening with the RS emblem in the center. The covers (or "doors") were powered electrically. The parking lamps were integrated into the lower valance. On the front fenders and rear, RS emblems appeared, along with black body stripes below the body side moldings.

The third package was the Super Sport, the performance model. The front grille bore an SS emblem in the center of the black grille and the hood featured a raised central area with simulated louvers. A wide "bumblebee" paint band wrapped around the front panel and the nose, identifying this F-car as an SS. At the rear, the gas filler cap had an SS badge, as did the steering wheel horn button. Either the standard 350 or optional 396 engine badges were displayed on the lower front fender behind the wheel openings. The taillamp panel was finished in flat black. Since the SS was the top performance option, the front and rear suspension components were beefed up with the F41 package and a heavy-duty radiator was included.

Option packages could be stacked together, allowing the RS and SS packages to be combined, providing the buyer with the blacked-out RS grille and the SS performance package.

The F-car was also offered with a bevy of performance options. Front disc brakes were new to GM products (except Corvette) in 1967 as well as the new F-car. Fast ratio steering with or without power assist was available, as was limited slip Posi-traction differential. The 9.5-inch diameter drum brakes could be ordered with sintered-metallic brake linings. A tachometer was a dealer-installed accessory.

As the new Chevrolet F-car was taking form and definition, one major marketing aspect was still undefined—the product's name. "Such absence of even a hint of a name might be considered unusual this late in the process," noted *Car Life*, "but in this case, it only serves to empha-

Out in the sunshine, this early Panther Rally Sport prototype has leaping Panther emblem and wrong striping.

Front view of Panther
Rally Sport shows
lack of parking lamps
in front valance.

Headlamp doors were pow-
ered by electric motors and
slid inwards behind grille to
expose headlamps.

size that pre-production work has been conducted at a relatively low
level of interest." Product planners and Chevrolet management had
combed hundreds of possible names, including Chevette, Nova,
Chaparral, Wildcat, and even GeMini (which also would be considered
for the Vega later) before settling on Panther. In June 1966, the name
Panther was retired and replaced by the name Camaro. "I went in a
closet," joked Chevrolet General Manager Pete Estes, "shut the door
and didn't come out until I had thought up a name." Chevrolet Public
Relations found an obscure French–English dictionary from 1935 that
translated Camaro as "comrade, pal or chum." The press had other versions, including "shrimp."

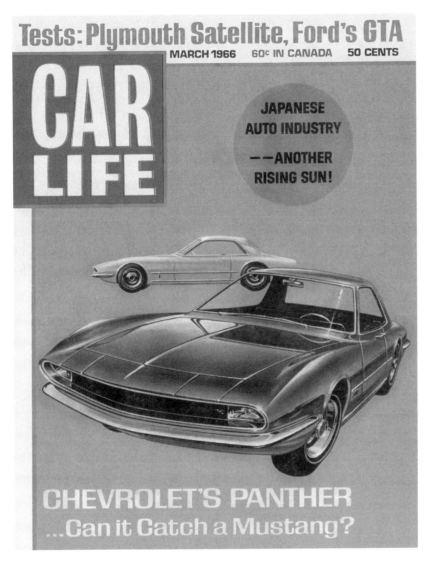

The automotive press grew ever more impatient waiting for Chevrolet to release its version of the Mustang. Car Life's March 1966 issue was critical of GM for taking too long to release the Camaro and not really caring about the car or the market it was to compete in.

Even before the car was introduced, Chevrolet was already taking criticism for waiting so long to release the F-car. "When Chevrolet unveils its new sporty compact this fall," noted *Car Life* in the March 1966 issue, "the one familiarly referred to as the Panther, it probably should be called the Reluctant Dragon. It has been reluctant to arrive, its creators seem reluctant to build it and the parent division is reluctant to admit its own 2-year delay in recognizing this spectacular segment of the automotive market."

While some of *Car Life*'s criticism was justified, resistance to the idea of another car line in the Chevrolet product lineup had some justification. The Chevy II had just been introduced in 1962 to compete directly against the Falcon while the Corvair was spinning off

In July 1966 *Motor Trend* teased readers with renderings of what the Camaro might look like. What they failed to blurb on the cover was inside—they had accurate spy shots of the real Camaro.

into more of an upscale, sporty car, far different from its compact car roots of 1960. When the Mustang first hit the market in April 1964, Chevrolet management still believed in the Corvair and its ability to compete with Ford's ponycar. They could not have been more wrong in their assessment. The Mustang had tapped a market that had only recently emerged and that GM had completely failed to envision. This new market was comprised of young men and women who wanted a car that was different from what their parents drove, something with verve and excitement and sporty looks. Ford quickly understood the diversity of this customer base by offering a base

Mustang to women ("Six And The Single Girl!" pronounced one Mustang ad) while commissioning Carroll Shelby to build the race-ready, brute-strong GT350.

Ford was able to get a substantial head start in the ponycar market, selling nearly 1.5 million Mustangs from mid-1964 to August 1966, before General Motors management gave the okay to develop its own version. Once the GM behemoth slowly began to gather momentum and all were in agreement that a Mustang-fighter was necessary, the F-car was the result, taking 25 months from approval of the proposal to its release on September 29, 1966.

When the enthusiast magazines hit the newsstands in late August with coverage of the new Camaro, they were mixed in their reviews. *Car Life* noted that "the speculators (*CL* included), who said the Camaro was to be a 'modified Chevy II' were wrong. It isn't. It's virtually a new car, just the way the Chevelle was a new car for 1964."

Hot Rod found the new Camaro "neat" but pondered the challenge Chevrolet had in breaking into a market owned by Ford. "You'd be surprised," *Hot Rod's* Eric Dahlquist noted, "how many people, even in a metropolis like Los Angeles, didn't know what a Camaro is, despite the formidable ad campaign that launched the car. We were amazed to learn that many thought our Bolero Red test car was a new Corvair or (Chevy stylists, clap your ears) a '67 Mustang, for goshsakes."

Driving the 1967 Camaro, which was optioned with the RS and SS packages, Dahlquist wrote, "The Camaro went like blue blazes—around the corner or in the straights—it made no difference…just pure sweetness to negotiate a bend at twice the normal velocity and still be master of the situation." They found the Camaro SS to be a well-balanced package that handled and accelerated superbly. The one fault found was the monoleaf springs, which tended to wind up when launched.

While the enthusiast press and the driving public reacted positively to the Camaro, some Chevrolet engineers weren't completely happy with the new car. "The car wasn't as smooth and vibration-free as we would have liked it," said Paul King, "but a lot of that had to do with product evolution. Part of those problems could also be attributed to the short development time allotted to the F-car." Fortunately, many of the problems that King and other engineers were aware of would be worked out in the 1968 and 1969 models.

Looking back on the first Camaro, Dave Holls, who was at that time Group Chief Designer, remembers, "The first car was such a compromise. And we were so concerned because the Mustang was such a statement. And for GM not to come out with something better was really difficult for us to take. When the Camaro came out we felt so much better. People just loved it and the dealers were crazy about the car. We had these little

1967 Camaro Production
June to December 1966

The first 1967 Camaro pilot cars were assembled at the Lordstown, Ohio and Van Nuys, California plants beginning on May 17, 1966, and completed on June 5. These cars were for use by Chevrolet's Public Relations for distribution to enthusiast magazines for road tests, internal GM use, and Chevrolet Engineering. By August 7, line workers and engineers had worked out assembly process glitches, and production ramped up to adequately supply dealers with cars for the Camaro's release at the end of September.

Month	Production Numbers
June	29
July	12
August	2830
September	12,876
October	21,302
November	29,497
December	27,871

Sandwiched between two big Chevys at the Norwood plant, this base V8 Camaro is on the trim line in the last phases of assembly.

yellow ones with the black bumblebee stripe going around the front—people bought them like crazy! It was an absolute winner."

Chevrolet Marketing took some novel approaches to bringing the Camaro story to the public using a variety of media. First came *The Camaro*, a 30-minute color movie about Chevrolet's new ponycar narrated by Milton Caniff (creator of "Steve Canyon," a popular action comic strip of the time) and featuring appearances by Chevrolet Designer Dave Holls, Engineer Don McPherson, Chief Engineer Alex Mair, and General Manager Bob Lund. *The Camaro* appeared in Detroit area theaters and was also broadcast on television.

In September, Chevrolet commissioned a stage production of *Off Broadway* performed by four different companies that played to 25 different cities in the United States and Canada through the fall of 1967. The stars of the stage were a pair of Camaros, one hardtop and one convertible, surrounded by an orchestra, dancers, and a chorus, all celebrating America's newest fun car. Chevrolet later admitted it had laid, as *Variety* would say, "an egg." History can at least credit Chevrolet for attempting a rather novel approach to marketing the Camaro against the entrenched and highly popular Mustang.

In the automotive marketing game, cross-marketing was—and continues to be—a popular and successful means to gain the buying public's attention. To establish a more sophisticated, avante garde image,

SS350 Camaro rises out of the primordial steam at its long-lead press debut in June 1966.

Percentage of Factory Installed Equipment—1967 Camaro

Automatic transmission	56.2
Four-speed transmission	21.5
V8 Engine	73.4
Six-cylinder engine	26.6
AM radio	78.8
Air conditioning	12.8
Tilt column	3.6
Power steering	41.7
Power drum brakes	8.3
Disc brakes	6.7
Power windows	2.2
Bucket seats	97.0
Vinyl top	23.7
White sidewall tires	63.0
Tinted windshield	37.1
Tinted windows/windshield	15.7
Dual exhaust	16.3
Limited slip differential	14.4
Wheel covers	67.9
Speed regulating device	0.1

Chevrolet, in conjunction with a leading New York fashion designer, released a line of women's clothes known as the Camaro Collection. The line was distributed to over 450 shops and was priced between $20 and $40.

The end result to all this hoopla was a pretty impressive new car arrival. Total sales for 1967 topped out at 220, 917 (roughly 10 percent of total Chevrolet sales that year). The RS option sold 64,842 units, and the

Above: Early clay proposal for Camaro convertible. Note absence of vent windows and radius of wheel openings.

Left: SS396 Camaro convertible in Deepwater Blue. Bright moldings around wheel openings and lower rocker panel were standard with the RS or SS packages.

SS recorded sales of 34, 411. Buyers preferred the V8 three to one over the six, no surprise since the sixties was the heyday of the V8 engine.

Did the new Camaro put a dent in the Mustang's sales success story? Ford pushed 472,121 Mustangs over the curb in 1967, down from the 1966 total of 607,568. Unfortunately, Chevrolet can't take total credit for the one-third decline in Mustang sales. New corporate cousin Mercury Cougar snared 150,893 customers, and Plymouth's restyled Barracuda sold 62,533 units. Far behind was the AMC Marlin, with only 2,545 copies sold.

The ponycar market was getting crowded, and, while Mustang still led the field, Ford could feel the pressure of competition. The ponycar market accounted for nearly 8.5 percent of sales in 1967, and a whole new generation of super ponycars was just over the horizon. These new cars included some with pavement-pounding big blocks and others with high-winding, small-displacement engines. Confident of their product, Chevrolet still faced strong marketing and promotional challenges to change America's mind that the Mustang wasn't the best ponycar. The ponycar wars were just starting to heat up.

Rally Sport with base 327 V8 in Bolero Red and black vinyl top. UPC 12 rally wheels are also installed.

Camaro Sets the Pace

The 1964 $^1/_2$ Mustang was chosen to pace the 1964 Indy 500, so it was no surprise that the new Camaro would get the nod to handle the pace car duties in 1967. As was the norm, Chevrolet supplied the Indianapolis Speedway with 81 white SS Camaro convertibles with Bright Blue custom interiors to be used as festival cars for parades and other activities during the event. The actual breakdown was 43 cars for the Indy 500 Committee, 25 for "VIP" use, 10 for Speedway use, and the 3 actual pace cars. Most of the festival cars were equipped with the L48 350 engine, while the L78 396/375 horsepower engine powered the three pace cars. Only one of the three cars was used to pace the race, driven by former Indy 500 winner and Chevrolet engineering consultant Mauri Rose.

A. J. Foyt won the race and, in usual Indianapolis tradition, was presented with the pace car, which he refused to accept since it wasn't equipped with air conditioning or power top. What is not widely known is Chevrolet built Foyt another pace car. It was part of a special order of 21 pace car replicas for shipment to Canada. These 21 cars (10 L48s and 11 L35) were built the last week of June 1967.

The Camaro was chosen to pace the 51st running of the Indianapolis 500 May 30 1967. The 396-powered Camaros had been well modified and fine-tuned to lead the pack at speeds in excess of 120 mph.

Above: Thirty-one of the seventy-eight 1967 Camaro pace car replicas park in a reserved field at the Indianapolis Motor Speedway. Three more Camaros were at Indy to serve as the real pacers.

Right: All pacers and replicas were painted Dover White with Bright Blue custom interiors. After the race, the cars ended up in the hands of dealers, mostly in the Midwest, for sale to the public. One of the original pace cars is in the basement of the Indianapolis Motor Speedway museum.

What It Took to Build a Pace Car

The origins of the three 1967 Camaro Indy 500 pace cars can be traced to Chevrolet Engineering Build Order Number 99168 dated March 30, 1967. Three Central Office Sales Department vehicles, all equipped with L78 396 cid engines were sent to the Experimental Department for modifications. Four sets of heavy-duty duty service front and rear springs were to be shipped with the cars "for possible vehicle installation if deemed necessary."

Cars 99168-A (the actual pace car) and 99168-B (according to internal Chevrolet records, 99168-C was never built) each received the following modifications and upgrades:

1. Change power train combination from "as delivered status" to RPO L35—396 V8 engine—M40 Turbo Hydra-Matic incorporating 3.07 ratio Positraction rear axle assembly (Garage).

2. Engines to be disassembled—visual checked by H. G. Sood and B. G. Stevens and reassembled for Test Lab OC-10 run-in (2 cycles—20 hrs.). Close attention to be given to running clearances toward high limit of production specifications, wrist pin clearances of .0003–.0004, piston to bore clearances of .0018–.0022, and mean to high limit bearing clearances. Pushrods should be 3/8 diameter with matching guide plate. RPO L-34-type piston rings and bearings to be installed as required. RPO L-34 camshaft, valve springs, etc. also to be installed if directed by R. L. Keinath.

3. All chassis safety items such as front suspension, steering linkage, etc. are to be magnafluxed (W. E. Minnick to coordinate).

4. Transmission assembly and rear axle assembly to be torn down, qualified and reassembled (E-A-T).

5. HD service metallic type brakes to be installed (if necessary) and spare shoes provided (W. E. Minnick to coordinate).

6. Heavy-duty duty service treatment to be given to items such as steering knuckles, ball studs, axle shafts, steering linkages, etc., and rear suspension if so deemed necessary by Chassis Design Engineers (E.L. Nash And C.M. Rubly) (W.E. Minnick to coordinate).

7. Balance prop shaft and wheel and tire assemblies. Spare wheel and tire assembles (three sets) to be provided. Magnaflux "U" joints and companion flanges. W.E. Minnick to provide spare tires (Test Car).

8. RPO N61 "deep tone" exhaust system to be installed as required (Garage).

9. Base ratio power steering to be installed as required (Garage).

10. HD battery and largest capacity alternator assembly to be installed and complete electrical system checked out. Premium belts to be installed at all locations, namely alternator, fan, etc. (Garage).

11. Maximum cooling capacity radiator to be installed in order to minimalize cooling problems (Garage).

Along with these mechanical upgrades, the shop was ordered to safety check the vehicles for ride and handling. "Show quality paint and interior trim is a basic requirement for all vehicles." Each of the pace cars had to be capable of running at 120–130 mph for the starting function.

Rear view of fastback proposal dated July 8, 1966 shows radical sweep from C pillars and Kammback treatment. The hatch would open to allow access to luggage compartment. The idea was to go head to head with Mustang's fastback. Dodge Charger and Barracuda also had fastbacks in their lineup. Chevrolet management wasn't sold on the idea and the fastback Camaro died in the styling studio.

Chapter Three
1968—Refining the Package

Since the Camaro was brand new for 1967, the second year of production was destined for refinement as engineering and the assembly plants continued to work the glitches out of the car. Also, in line with General Motors product planning, several new accessories and standard equipment additions were made. Although the changes made to the 1968 Camaro were minor, the Van Nuys and Norwood plants were shut down for three weeks from July 7 to July 28 for annual

There had been some industry talk that Ford would produce a station wagon version of the Mustang. That prompted styling to do a Camaro station wagon concept. Rear view shows lift-open hatch to access luggage compartment. Forward leaning B pillar was reminiscent of 1955–1957 Nomad station wagon series.

Above: Designers were toying with several locations for Camaro badge. This study has Camaro nameplates both in the grille and on the front fenders directly behind SS emblem. Production models had nameplate at top of header panel on left-hand side.

model year changeover. Production then resumed, and dealers began showing the 1968 Camaro on September 21, 1967.

Despite some difficulty in winning the public's attention away from the Mustang, GM management was satisfied with the 1967 Camaro's sales results. Those within Product Planning and Marketing analyzed which Chevrolet car line the Camaro would most severely cut into when it was introduced. Industry pundits had predicted the Corvair would suffer the most damage in the showroom. The 1967 Corvair and

Right: Unusual addition to this proposal is an air extractor located behind the front wheel openings.

Custom interior with N34 wheel, air conditioning and very rare A31 power windows. Less than one percent were equipped with power windows in 1968.

Custom interior with RPO N34 wood grained steering wheel, U57 eight-track stereo tape player and floor-mounted Muncie shifter.

its sporty image went head to head with the new Camaro, but the negative press initiated by Ralph Nader's book *Unsafe at Any Speed* and the lack of a V8 engine had doomed the Corvair. To illustrate how significant the damage had been to the Corvair's image and position, a three-year comparison of sales explains how the bottom literally fell out of the Corvair:

Year	Production
1965	235,500
1966	103,743
1967	27,253

In retrospect, the decision in August 1964 to build a Mustang competitor was correct for more reasons than originally anticipated. No one knew at that time how strong the ponycar market would become by the end of the decade. Nor did GM foresee the blitzkrieg of negative press resulting from the Nader expose that, almost overnight, would torpedo any hopes of saving the Corvair. Consequently, the new Camaro filled voids not anticipated by GM management.

Those who felt the Camaro would infringe on sales of the Chevy II were proved wrong. Sales of the Chevy II remained consistent from

1968 Camaro Base Prices

Body	Engine	Price
2 dr. Hardtop	L6	$2421
2 dr. Hardtop	V8	$2521
2 dr. Convertible	L6	$2624
2 dr. Convertible	V8	$2724

the boom year of 1965 when Chevrolet's compact accounted for 4.9 percent of total Division sales, jumping to 5.7 percent in 1966 as overall Division sales dropped 7.5 percent, and remaining at 5.6 percent against the Camaro in its inaugural year. Although Division sales took a tumble of over 315,000 units in 1967, the Chevy II held strong at 106,000 sold. Obviously, the Chevy II was unaffected by the introduction of the Camaro.

Since the Camaro was all new in 1967, the second year of production would only deal with refinements and corrections. Changes would also be made to bring the Camaro in line with GM's across-the-board refinements as well as addressing safety and emissions regulations. These corrections had been preplanned for installation in GM vehicles across the board and included new emission controls, side marker lamps, and flow-through ventilation.

Side marker lamps were added to the flanks of the 1968 Camaro, located in the front fender ahead of the wheel opening and in the rear quarter, just ahead of the bumper wraparound. A controlled-combustion emission system was utilized in Camaros equipped with Powerglide transmissions. All manual and Hydra-Matic equipped cars used A.I.R. (air injection reactor) equipment. Most significant was the introduction of Astro flow-through ventilation. A new addition to almost every GM model, Astro Ventilation flowed air through the passenger compartment through vents in the instrument panel and exited out through ducts located beneath the door pillar panel. Flow-through ventilation pleased stylists because they no longer had to deal with the unsightly ventiplanes. A new curved one-piece glass gave the Camaro's profile a cleaner appearance. It also pleased the bean counters since it was no longer necessary to carry two different instrument panels in inventory, one for air conditioning and one without. Now one instrument panel could suffice for both applications. Smokers used to knock-

Custom interior with N34 steering wheel, D55 console, and U17 gauge package. Note location of tachometer and clock integrated in right-hand pod. "Horseshoe" shifter was used with automatic transmission models beginning in 1968.

Base interior. Gauges under dash and tachometer located on steering column are representative of what owners installed in their Camaros in the sixties. Flow through ventilation ducts can be found on each end of the panel.

ing their cigarette ashes out the vent window as they drove had to learn to use the ashtray.

Other refinements included a minor redesign of the center console and the optional console gauge package (RPO U17). The gauge faces were changed from circular to rectangular and clustered in two tiers consisting of oil pressure and fuel, water temperature and ammeter. While the clock was part of the package, it wasn't located in the cluster. Instead, it was integrated with the tachometer and placed in the right-hand instrument pod. Some have referred to this arrangement as the "Tic Toc Tac." The Strato Bench seat was again offered, as was new houndstooth cloth upholstery in black and white. The Z23 Special

RPO L34 350-horsepower SS396 added $350 to the sticker price. Air conditioning was available with either the 325 or 350 horsepower versions of the 396.

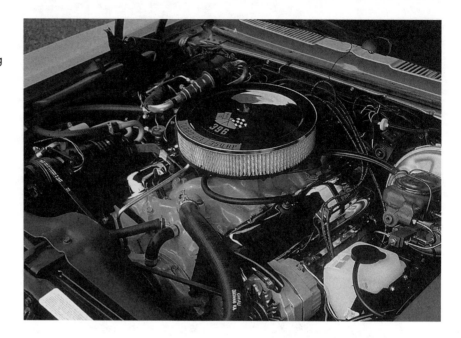

Interior Group now added simulated wood grain accents on the instrument panel. A passenger grab bar was installed above the glovebox door when either the Custom or Special Interior groups were ordered.

Another major change was the elimination of electric motors to open and close the hidden headlamp doors on Rally Sport and Rally Sport / Super Sport models. Both the Corvette and the Camaro shared vacuum componentry in 1968, in the Corvette it was used to open and close the headlamp assemblies and in the Camaro it was employed to operate the headlamp doors. Although performance was only as good as the integrity of the vacuum hoses and canisters, it was an improvement over the electric doors, which could freeze up during extreme cold weather.

To handle the additional punishment of extreme driving, Chevrolet added the heavy-duty M22 Rockcrusher close-ratio four-speed manual gearbox. And while four-wheel disc brakes were not offered as an RPO, a customer could either have the dealer install the package or he could buy it over the counter and install it himself.

Perhaps the most significant modification to the 1968 Camaro was the rear suspension. The monoleaf springs with the shocks mounted ahead of the axle had proven to be exceptionally prone to windup and axle hop. "The single leaf spring was Ed Cole's idea," recalls chassis engineer Paul King. "The springs didn't have any interleaf damping or friction and that was both a curse and a blessing. The interleaf had a lot of bad things about it, one thing being you couldn't count on it being consistent as it aged and weathered because they would respond differ-

Styling proposal to emphasize V-angle of grille dated July 1, 1966. New front stripe mockup was also considered. Five-spoke mag wheel was considered and then dropped.

ently. But the single leaf spring had this "freedom of motion forever"—it just didn't have any damping in it. We had every kind of problem you could think of, including vibration modes and weird windup modes that were very detrimental to the car and the driveline."

When King watched high-speed movie film of the rear suspension in operation, he discovered the rear axle hop went not only up and down but also fore and aft. "It was almost like a whirling motion," King recalled. He suggested the rear shocks be staggered. While all the magazine road tests and reports coming back from customers complained about the windup, King remembers "As far as Chevrolet was concerned, the windup problems were discovered at the Proving Grounds."

Placing the left side shock behind the axle and the right side shock ahead, windup and axle tramp was significantly reduced. Further tests indicated that the antiwindup bar used on the 1967 rear suspension created more trouble than it corrected, so it was abandoned. Finally, multileaf springs were utilized for the L48 350 engine and all 396-engine applications. With these improvements, no further research was done on fitting the rear with an anti-sway bar.

No significant changes were made to the three Camaro packages—Standard, RS and SS. However, SS models equipped with the 396 engine received a blacked-out tail lamp panel. The RS package accounted for 40,977 sold, and the SS with its various engine choices sold 27,884 copies. The standard and optional six-cylinder and small-block

The L34 and L35 Turbo Jet 396 engines used iron block, heads, and intake manifold.

V8 engines were retained with few changes. Most significant was the new Torque Drive version of the two-speed Powerglide automatic transmission. With the Torque Drive, the driver could shift manually without the need for a clutch pedal. The real news came with the introduction of two additional packages for the 396 engine. First was the L34, rated at 350 horsepower @ 5200 rpm and 415 lb-ft of torque @ 3400 rpm and offered with all transmission choices. It also could be ordered with air conditioning.

Performance V8 Production

RPO	CID	HP	Production
L30	327	275	21,686
L48	350	295	12,496
L34	396	350	2,579
L35	396	325	10,773
L78	396	375	4,575
L89	396	375	272

Two versions of the 375-horsepower 396 were offered. Both had a compression ratio of 11.00:1 and were rated at 375 horsepower @ 5600 rpm and torque of 415 lb-ft @ 3600 rpm. Both could be ordered with the heavy-duty three-speed manual or M20, M21, or M22 four-speed transmissions. No automatic transmission was offered with this pair of solid lifter big blocks. The primary difference between the L78 and the L89 version was their cylinder heads—the L78's was cast alloy iron while the L89's was aluminum alloy.

Cosmetically, exteriors were little changed for 1968. On SS350 models, the hood was carried over from 1967; however, SS396 versions sported a special hood with simulated carburetor stacks. Around front, the grille was given a more pronounced center angle on SS and standard models. The RS grille was unchanged. Standard and SS models (without the RS package) received backup lamps within the tail lamp lens assemblies separated by bright molding. On RS models the backup lamps moved to below the rear bumper.

The ponycar market had continued to evolve in 1968. Overall sales for the segment were down almost 9 percent (close to 115,000 cars) from 1967. The field was tightening up as the six ponycars from GM, Ford, and Chrysler fought for a piece of the sales pie. American Motors' new Javelin and the exciting two-seat AMX were rifle shots directly to the heart of the market and provided AMC with a larger slice of ponycar profits.

Even the L78 had to endure the strangulating A.I.R. emissions system. The 375-horsepower L78 shown here boasted an aluminum intake manifold and big Holley carburetor. Cast iron exhaust manifolds were as close to headers as the factory could build.

Rear view of D80 ducktail spoiler. According to Chevrolet Research and Development engineer Paul Van Valkenburg, the Camaro's spoiler package was one of the most effective to come out of the Detroit. Van Valkenburg had the opportunity to fine-tune the spoilers in the windtunnel in 1966.

Grotto Blue 1968 RS/SS396 sports white vinyl top and restyled accent stripe streaming back from front accent band.

SS396 in Island Teal. Note engine displacement is now located on front of fender inside front accent band. Grille and rear tail lamp panel are blacked out with SS package.

At the Drags

Chevrolet racers continued to modify the new Camaros, dialing in the suspension and chassis for better launches and building stronger engines. As they did, they began to dominate some of the Super Stock classes. At the 1968 NHRA Winternationals at Pomona, California, Bill "Grumpy" Jenkins took the SS/C class in his Camaro, recording a 11.18/125.87 mph. In C/Stock, Ben Wenzel grabbed the class win with his 1968 Camaro, turning a 12.46/112.64 mph.

Later that summer at the NHRA Nationals in Indianapolis, Indiana, Jenkins continued his domination of the SS/C class, grabbing the win with a 11.48/116.27 mph. Another 1968 Camaro, driven by Ernie Musser, nabbed the SS/F class with a 12.77/85.95 mph. In the higher classes, Hill & Arons' 1968 took the SS/EA class with a 11.91/104.89 mph. In SS/FA, Edgel McClelland took the class with a 12.33/112.64 mph.

Exterior and Interior Trim Codes

Exterior Colors	Accent Stripes	Standard Interior Sport Coupe & Convertible				Custom Interior Sport Coupe & Convertible									Custom Interior Sport Coupe			
		Black	Blue	Gold	Red	Black	Blue	Gold	Black	Blue	Gold	Red	Turq.	Parch.	Black	Blue	Turq.	B&W*
Tuxedo Black	White	E	B	G	D	E	B	G	E	B	G	D	T	K	E	B	T	Q
Ermine White		E	B	G	D	E	B	G	E	B	G	D	T	K	E	B	T	Q
Grotto Blue		E	B			E	B		E	B				K	E	B		Q
Fathom Blue		E	B			E	B		E	B				K	E	B		Q
Island Teal		E				E			E					K	E			Q
Ash Gold		E		G		E		G	E		G			K	E			Q
Grecian Green		E				E			E					K	E			Q
Tripoli Turquoise		E				E			E				T	K	E		T	Q
Teal Blue		E	B			E	B		E	B				K	E	B		Q
Cordovan Maroon		E			D	E			E			D		K	E			Q
Seafrost Green		E				E			E					K	E			Q
Matador Red		E			D	E			E			D		K	E			Q
Palomino Ivory		E		G		E		G	E		G			K	E			Q
Sequoia Green		E		G		E		G	E		G			K	E			Q
Butternut Yellow		E		G		E		G	E		G			K	E			Q

Trim Codes:

B	Blue	E	Black
K	Parchment	Q	Black/White*
T	Turquoise	G	Gold
D	Red		

Houndstooth cloth

SS396 in Corvette Bronze. Note standard hubcaps and location of parking lamps in blacked-out grille. RS models placed parking lamps in valance. Front accent band now extended back in one flowing line and then tapered back to door. Camaro nameplate and engine callout are contained within the accent stripe.

Ash Gold RS/SS with D80 rear spoiler and over the counter front spoiler.

This ad highlights options available to tailor the Camaro to the buyer's desires and requirements. In many respects, this ad is in response to Mustang's claim to have an extensive option and accessory list.

Customizing the Camaro.

Take a Camaro, any Camaro. Add sport striping that straddles the nose and leaps down both flanks. A spoiler on the deck. White-stripe tires, mag-spoke wheel covers. Pick a bold color borrowed from Corvette: Bronze, British Green, LeMans Blue; or new Rallye Green. Now order 325 hp under a stacked hood, the 4-speed, houndstooth-checked upholstery, AM-FM multiplex stereo radio and/or tape. If that's still not enough customizing, see your Chevy dealer. He's got the book.

CHEVROLET

Camaro SS Coupe with customizing sport trim.

See How They Ran—Big-Block Style

RPO	HP	Carb	Trans	0–60	Quarter Mile	Magazine
L35	325	QJ	THM	6.6	15.0/93.9 mph	*C&D* 3/68
L35	325	QJ	THM	7.8	15.6/92.0 mph	*MT* 1/68
L78	375	H	4M	—	14.09/99.0 mph	*PHR* 2/68

C&D = Car and Driver   MT = Motor Trend   PHR = Popular Hot Rodding

Percentage of Factory Installed Equipment— 1968 Camaro

Automatic transmission	56.4
Four-speed transmission	20.2
V8 Engine	78.3
Six-cylinder engine	21.6
AM radio	81.9
Air conditioning	15.2
Tilt column	2.2
Power steering	49.0
Power drum brakes	18.8
Disc brakes	8.5
Power windows	0.1
Bucket seats	97.9
Vinyl top	32.7
White sidewall tires	60.0
Tinted windshield	25.8
Tinted windows/windshield	27.7
Limited slip differential	15.6
Wheel covers	56.8
Speed regulating device	0.1

Model	Production
Javelin/AMX	58,849
Mustang	317,148
Cougar	113,726
Barracuda	45,412
Firebird	107,112
Camaro	235,151

The SS Camaro stands shoulder to shoulder with big brother 1968 Corvette. Tying the Camaro to the Corvette and letting the sportcar's halo shine on the Camaro's performance image was a ploy Ford could not utilize with the Mustang.

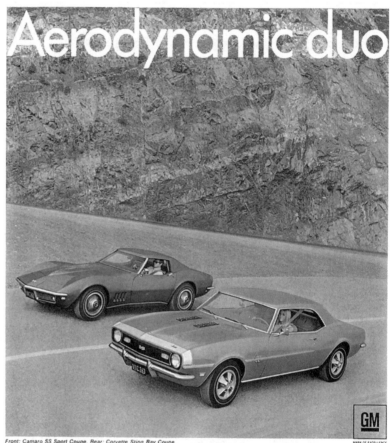

Front: Camaro SS Sport Coupe. Rear: Corvette Sting Ray Coupe.   MARK OF EXCELLENCE

They're two of a kind. The fantastic, low-slung Corvette Sting Ray. And Camaro, The Hugger, the only car that comes even close. In styling, in handling, in performance. Both are aerodynamic from nose to deck, with Astro Ventilation, full door-glass styling, bucket seats, refined suspension and 327-cu.-in. standard V8s. You can order Vettes all the way up to 435 hp in a 427-cu.-in. Turbo-Jet V8. Camaros score almost as high: Cubes — 396. Horses — 325. Corvette's a tough act to follow. Buckle up a Camaro and see what we've done for an encore.

Camaro '68 CHEVROLET **Corvette**

After enjoying three years of phenomenal sales, the Mustang was now feeling the effect of its success as buyers wandered off to compare other models like Mercury's Cougar. The Cougar had tapped some of the Mustang's sales volume as the ponycar market expanded and customers were more attracted to the idea of a personal luxury car. It didn't matter if equipped with a six, small V8, or a ground-pounding big cube rocket, the ponycar and its muscle car big brother were the hottest segments in the automotive marketplace.

Even though the ponycar segment contracted in 1968, the Camaro actually gained market share, climbing from 22.2 percent in 1967 to 26.8 percent in 1968. Mustang sales had tumbled considerably as the Camaro offered more options, packages, and engine choices for the ponycar buyer. Chevrolet management was satisfied that the Camaro had begun to make inroads into the Mustang's sales volume, and, at nearly 11 percent of total Chevrolet production, the Camaro was maturing nicely into Chevrolet's product lineup.

By December 1966, another front-end design had surfaced, this one with a decidedly European influence. The stripes are close to the ones used in production in 1969. The problem with this proposal was it would be stuck on the high Chevy II cowl. The proportions simply weren't right.

Chapter Four
1969—Caught in the Corporate Design Wars

After posting successful sales records in 1967 and 1968, the Camaro entered its third year of production with new sheet metal and a growing reputation among performance enthusiasts. Chevrolet's strategy to emphasis the Camaro's brawn was in keeping with the high-performance market in the late sixties. It was the heyday of big cube engines in both musclecars like the SS396 Chevelle and the SS350 and SS396 Camaro. Chevrolet also tied the Camaro to the Corvette's aura, buying ad space in many enthusiast magazines showing the two cars together and suggesting the subtle message that the Camaro was born to be the Corvette's younger sibling.

How the Camaro had been packaged and accessorized had worked superbly in 1967–1968, and Chevrolet Product Planning had no intention of fixing what wasn't broken. The Camaro again came in three packages—Standard, Rally Sport, and Camaro Super Sport, all equipped with the Standard Interior, Special Interior Group (RPO Z23), or Custom Interior (RPO Z87). The SS could be ordered with either the Style Trim Group (Z21) or the RS package (RPO Z22).

While the basic packages were similar to previous years, that's about where the similarities end between the 1967–1968 and the 1969 Camaros. While most of the structural engineering of the earlier cars was carried over, the 1969 Camaro received revised sheet metal; improvements to chassis, brakes and suspension; and revised interiors and trim. Some segments of the powertrain were upgraded, the base 327 engine was changed to a 307, and a second version of the 350-cubic inch engine was offered.

This "Kin to Corvette" ad portrayed the image Chevorlet had cultivated for the Camaro. The Hugger Orange paint, 396 big block, variable steering, big wheels and tires and the message that there was a little Corvette in every Camaro.

'69 Camaro SS Sport Coupe with RS equipment and new Corvette Coupe

We'll take on any other two cars in the magazine.

Camaro SS, plus Rally Sport.
Black grille.
Undercover headlights with built-in water jets to clean them.
Up to 325 hp on order.
Sport stripes.
Special hood.
Power disc brakes.
Seven-inch rims and wide oval tires made very obvious with raised white lettering.
Head restraints.
New Hurst-linkage 4-speed available.

Can't be driven when steering column is locked.
Usually seen in the company of people who can tell the real article from an imitation.
Known as "The Hugger."
Kin to Corvette.
Corvette, 'Vette, Stingray and other sassy names.
Unusually powerful looking hood.
Morocco-grain vinyl on instrument panel.
New map pockets.

Wider 8-inch wheels.
New assist grips on the doors.
Six bucket seat colors.
New concealed door handles.
Built-in headlight washers.
The driver of this car is always ready with 350 cubic inches of new standard V8.
Other cars, if we were you, we'd drive on the other side of the street.
Way on the other side.

Putting you first, keeps us first.

While the external changes to the 1969 Camaro were evolutionary, the really radical concepts were left on the boards or in clay at Chevrolet's Design Studio II. Initially, the plan in 1966 was to provide the 1969 Camaro with all new sheet metal. "We thought we were going to get new sheet metal for 1969," recalls designer Dave Holls, "but when we found out that we were going to use the same cowl and windshield, then we got into some rather awkward stuff as we tried to rework the old package." Holls, who worked with Henry Haga at Design Staff, remembers, "It was harder to rework the old package, with its short dash to axle and high cowl, which was all done off the Nova."

What's "Z" Option Code?

An RPO number identified Regular Production Options (RPOs). Usually, General Motors categorized options by RPO. For example, all engine RPOs started with the letter *L*, transmissions used *M*, and brakes started with a *J*.

The Z series was used primarily for model options and groups:

Z21   Style Trim Group

Z22   Rally Sport package

Z23   Special Interior Group

Z87   Custom Interior

Z27   Camaro SS

Z28   Special Performance Package

Many enthusiasts believed that the Z28 option was named after Chief Corvette Engineer Zora Arkus-Duntov, but the RPO was chosen since it numerically followed the Z27 SS option. While it takes some of the myth out of the RPO, the Z28 was a legend in its own right.

Alex Mair, who was Chevrolet's Chief Passenger Car Engineer at the time, remembers, "Fairly early on in the 1969 model development, we knew the car was not going to be all new because work on the 1970 car was already underway, and that was a totally redesigned car. The changes on the '69 had originally been perceived as being greater than they ended up. The Camaro did get a facelift, not a major change because the 1970 car was coming along. At that time it wasn't going to be ready, so it was introduced as a 1970 $^1/_2$."

Chevrolet designers were anxious to change the Camaro's sheet metal and grabbed at the opportunity to revise the Camaro's exterior. Two schools emerged in Chevrolet's design studio. One group worked from a clean sheet that involved a lower cowl, increased windshield rake, and lower roofline. The other school retained the higher cowl and less windshield rake and attempted to graft lower rooflines and higher quarterpanel kickups to make the car look lower. Some of the concepts were taken directly from the Corvette. "As you look at the concept clays," notes Dave Holls, "there's a mixture of those styling elements we wanted so bad but were so difficult to merge with the old architecture of awkward high roofs and cowls and the short front. Some of those looks we couldn't really do, and that's why we lost a lot of those front and rear ideas to a more conventional design—they just worked better. Rather than come out with something dumb, it was better to come out with something like your previous cars than to do that."

Above: Within Chevrolet's Design Studio, there were two approaches to the sheetmetal on the 1969 Camaro. Early on, it was thought the Camaro would no longer be married to the Chevy II's architecture, allowing stylists to drop the high cowl and lower the roofline. This comparison of a 1968 production Camaro with a 1969 proposal shows the cars are similar below the beltline but the proposal has a severely raked windshield.

Right: This is the clay that appears with the production Camaro in the proceeding photo in the courtyard at Chevrolet's Design Center. The lower cowl and faster windshield are clearly evident in this clay.

Fighting the Corporate Design Wars

There's no mystery here, nor were there any hidden agendas—nothing more than meets the eye. The 1969 Camaro facelift was a normal "styling versus the corporate program," which always worked this way:

1. Start "void"—all new windshield, cowl, roof, and lower sheet metal for proportions and lineage (Bill Mitchell hated the original Camaro because it had to be based on the Chevy II geometry). At the same time, Design was developing the "Corporate Program" facelift. The two directions went on at the same time, but in separate studios.

2. Develop both directions. Try to sell the "hot one" to management by making their mouths water in reviews and comparison showings. Fight for addition of a fastback (the Mustang had one) and a "shooting break" wagon.

3. After management decisions are made, collect the pieces and execute the final production design.

—*Chuck Jordon, GM Executive Designer*

By early 1967, the idea of any dramatic sheet metal changes or approval of a new roof and cowl had been ruled out. Instead, Design began refining the existing car, massaging the sheet metal while retaining the old, high-body Nova architecture. GM stylists were working on the next-generation F-car, and many of the themes and concepts found in the 1969 Camaro clays found their way onto the 1970 $^{1}/_{2}$ car. While the idea of a new Camaro for 1969 was an exciting prospect, it made no sense to design all new metal for a car that would have a production run of 18 months at most, only to be replaced by another all new model. The Camaro had quickly become a moneymaker for Chevrolet; however, management couldn't make a significant investment in the 1969 car. "The more money we put into the '69, the less we would have had to put into the '70 $^{1}/_{2}$," said Dave Holls. "It would have involved a longer time frame that the body would have had to run. All of it was a compromise."

Elements of the 1970 1/2 Camaro appear on this 1969 proposal using the Chaparral nameplate. The high cowl and window rake reveals it was a 1969 first design. This clay was an influence on the 1970 1/2 rear with Kammback and ducktail spoiler. Hanging a thin blade bumper on this car would have been easy at the time; only 7/10s of an inch protection was all that was necessary for the rear end.

Tail view of same clay shows smooth lines as C-pillar flows into the quarter panel and deck. Note studies of rear window rake and ducktail spoiler. Dave Holls remembers this body would have been used with the new roof if it had been approved.

Instead, the Camaro received a new, aggressive "loop" front-end treatment with a rectangular Argent Silver crosshatch plastic grille, bow tie emblem in the center, and single headlamps integrated into the grille. The parking lamps were located beneath the bumper in the front valance. A new option (RPO VE3) replaced the chrome front bumper with a resilient bumper made of urethane keyed to match the exterior color. The grille was painted black on SS models. When the RS option was ordered, the headlamps were hidden by doors and the grille was encircled by bright molding and an RS emblem was affixed in the cen-

This clay dated October 11, 1966 shows hood cutouts with engine displacement plates. The modified bumblebee stripe with the trailing tape treatment is reminiscent of the Shelby GT500. Bill Mitchell did not like vinyl roofs on Camaros, so designers toyed with several different approaches to what was a popular option.

New sheetmetal proposal dated November 13, 1966 shows loop style front end with recessed grille, hood vents, and raked windshield. If the new sheetmetal had been approved for 1969, this car would have been influential.

ter of the grille. The headlamp doors had three wide "slits" that allowed some light to shine through at night in case the vacuum-operated doors failed to operate. When the SS package was included, the grille was painted black and the SS emblem was used in the center of the grille. As part of the RS option, a vacuum-operated headlamp washer was standard and offered on all other models.

A spectacular new hood was offered for SS models (RPO ZL2). This metal hood featured a raised center, which extended back toward the cowl and the windshield. Chevrolet had used cowl induction in their

Above: This picture, taken December 21, 1966, shows the 1967 Camaro on the left; the center model is the proposal for a lower cowl and roof; and on the right is a model for new sheetmetal using the existing cowl and roof. Stylists wanted the center version; GM management wouldn't fund a major sheetmetal change for 1969.

Middle: Another very close version of what the 1969 Camaro might have been if the new roof and cowl had been granted. "It all clicked with this car," remembers designer Dave Holls. "Then we were told we couldn't have that roof because it literally changed all the sheetmetal."

Bottom: Another proposal for 1969, this one dated February 3, 1967, for a fastback Version. C pillar and upper quarters have a massive appearance that's out of place compared to the more delicate front end.

Above: Chevy stylists were pushing this proposal as the 1969 Camaro. Note the similarity to the Chevelle in the C pillar and quarterpanel. The lower roofline was dependent on a lower cowl. Front overhang is longer than production Camaro. Bill Mitchell took one look at this clay and said "Nice shot guys. You finally got yourselves two Chevelles." The clay soon disappeared.

Left: "Flow-through" rear end treatment on 1969 Camaro clay. This was rejected since it looked too much like regular passenger car lines.

racecars for years; however, this was only the second time it had been offered for street performance cars. A fiberglass cowl induction hood package was also offered over the counter to fit both cross ram dual quads or single four-barrel setups.

Above the left-hand headlamp on the header panel was a script nameplate reading "Camaro by Chevrolet." At the front of the front fenders was the engine displacement call-out (except for the base engine). Behind the front wheel openings was the model nameplate (Camaro on base models; Rally Sport and Super Sport when ordered).

By May of 1967 the die had been cast. The Camaro would only get a facelift while the big money would be spent on the 1970 1/2. This profile shows louvers in the front and rear fenders and a different vinyl roof treatment that used paint between the gutter and top trim to give it a lighter appearance. Door handles are precursors to 1969 Grand Prix.

A pronounced feature line began at the front of the wheel openings (front and rear) and streamed back, with the front line ending at the center of the door and the rear trailing to the end of the quarterpanel. Three false louvers trimmed with bright moldings were attached ahead of the rear wheel opening on all models except base cars (unless ordered with RPO Z21 Style Trim Group). At the rear, the quarterpanels flared out to give the Camaro a low, muscular appearance. On the right rear of the decklid another "Camaro by Chevrolet" nameplate appeared. The tail lamps were divided into three segments on all models except the RS models, which received horizontally segmented tail lamps with the backup lamps in the lower valance. In the center of the tail lamp panel was the model emblem. The tail lamp panel was blacked out on 396-equipped SS models. RPO D80 front and rear spoilers were available for all models.

Inside, the Camaro featured a new instrument panel and gauge cluster. The flow-through ventilation ducts were at the outboard ends of the panel. The gauge cluster was divided into three segments, with the speedometer in the left window, the clock in a smaller window above the steering column, and the fuel gauge in the right. On either side of the steering column were panels containing the switches for the headlamps, wipers, and radio. Above the radio were the vertically sliding controls for the HVAC. Another set of air vents were located at the top center of the panel with the ashtray directly below. A "Camaro" nameplate appeared above the ashtray, and the trimplate extended to the end of the panel. Beneath this trim panel was the glovebox. The standard two-spoke steering wheel had horn tabs on each end of the bar.

High front-end view of 1968 taken June 9, 1966 shows development of ZL2 cowl induction hood designed by Larry Shinoda. Note Panther nameplate in grille.

ZL2 cowl induction hood study, shown on 1968 SS396.

Right: Open hood view reveals air plenum integrated into underhood. Foam sealer around carburetor is also installed. The plenum and the foam would meet and seal hot underhood air from carburetor.

Bottom: SS350 engine compartment. Foam seal on air cleaner assembly mated to ZL2 "Super Scoop."

When the Custom Interior (RPO Z87) was ordered, simulated wood grain was applied to the center of the wheel spoke, the switch panel, and the ashtray and glovebox area. A passenger grab bar was also included in the package. And for the first time, the ignition switch was moved from the instrument panel to the steering column in accordance with new federal regulations.

A handsome three-spoke steering wheel with chrome spokes and plastic wood-grained rim was optional, as was the console-mounted Special Instrumentation (RPO U17). When ordered, fuel, ammeter, and oil pressure gauges were mounted in two staggered tiers. The clock and the tachometer were installed in the IP gauge cluster. When the automatic transmission was ordered with console, a "horseshoe" shifter was installed with the reverse détente lockout at the top of the shifter. Also, Hurst shifters were offered for the first time on manual transmission-equipped models.

The seats were redesigned, with integrated headrests and all vinyl upholstery. All models could be ordered with the Custom Interior, with ribbed inserts in the seat back and the seat cushion. With the Custom Interior, the door panels were molded and upgraded with door pull handles and armrests integrated into the panel. The third interior upgrade was the cloth houndstooth upholstery inserts on seat backs and seat cushions. This had first been introduced in 1968 in black and white; choices were now expanded to include a yellow houndstooth and an orange houndstooth pattern. The Custom Interior door panels were included when the houndstooth upholstery was ordered. The rear seat could be folded down for additional storage by specifying RPO A67.

This is as basic as it gets. Standard interior with floor shifter, no console or sport steering wheel. Optional factory tachometer is in right hand gauge pod.

Houndstooth interior was popular in 1969; colors offered were Ivory, Black, Yellow, or Orange. Houndstooth upholstery was only offered in Custom Interiors.

Underneath, the Camaro still utilized a unit body with separate front subframe. Chevrolet engineers continued to refine the subframe and its attachments to reduce road and engine noise in the passenger compartment. A new, variable-ratio power steering box required fewer turns lock-to-lock and provided better road feel at speed. While the standard drum brakes were essentially carried over, a new, single-caliper front disc brake was offered. Even better was the production release of four-wheel disc brakes (RPO JL8), which included multileaf rear springs, Positraction rear, and F70 x 15 belted tires. This was also the first year for EDP (Electronic Data Processing), a new procedure used by all GM divisions that "identified the correct spring for the weight of the vehicle including optional equipment ordered by the customer." According to GM, the EDP process "provided a smoother ride and better handling by computer matching spring to application." Also offered was the RPO F41 Special Performance Front and Rear Suspension that featured higher deflection springs and revalved shocks.

Computer spring selection or not, the rear suspension continued to be a chronic problem for big-block Camaros. Even though Chevrolet now utilized a wider five-leaf spring (2.80 inches compared to 2.25 inches for 1968), the deflection rate remained at 100 lb. per inch on 396-equipped models. *Car Life* found the revised rear springs to still be inadequate. "The rear suspension is plain vanilla, the weak linkage between axle and car, and it drags the 396 Camaro down to the level of just another Camaro."

Car Life also found the handling, braking, and cornering in the SS396 were downright treacherous. "At the mere suggestion of work, the axle leaps and hop, judders and bucks . . . starting, stopping or turn-

Custom interior option RPO Z87 included special door panels with molded armrests and wood grained accents on steering wheel, instrument panel and console.

Black houndstooth Custom Interior boasts rare Comfortilt steering column (6,575 ordered), air conditioning and wood grained accents.

ing, whatever the rest of the cars wants to do, the rear suspension won't let it do it." The revisions made in 1968 were adequate for the six-cylinder and small-block powertrains, but apply the big block's tremendous torque and the axle would crash against its mounts. Handling was also a so-so proposition. With almost 60 percent of the weight on the front wheels, cornering was all understeer, and as soon as the rear unloaded, the tires would lose adhesion and the SS396 would attempt to swap rears. "Power doesn't move the Camaro forward," *Car Life* noted, "it rotates the rest of the car around the engine." It was a problem that Chevrolet never would solve.

1969 Camaro Base Prices

Body	Engine	Price
2 dr. Hardtop	L6	$2621
2 dr. Hardtop	V8	$2726
2 dr. Convertible	L6	$2835
2 dr. Convertible	V8	$2940

If Camaro continued to have an advantage over all other ponycars, it was in the availability of engines. The base motor continued to be the 230-cubic inch, one-barrel Rochester inline six-cylinder rated at 140 horsepower and offered with a three-speed manual transmission standard and choices of optional four-speed manual, two-speed Powerglide, and, for the first time, the M40 Turbo Hydra-Matic. The other six-cylinder choice was the 150 horsepower L22 that displaced 250 cubes and featured a mild-lift camshaft for economy.

The standard V8 was the 210-horsepower 327 V8 with two-barrel Rochester carb, 9:0:1 compression, and 320 lb-ft of torque at 2400 rpm. During the middle of the 1969 model year, the 327 was discontinued in favor of a 200-horsepower small block displacing 307 cubes as the standard V8. Another new addition to the line was the 255-horsepower version of the 350 with lower compression and more moderate camshaft. It replaced the 275-horsepower 327. Next up was the 300-horsepower 350 engine with 10.25:1 compression, Rochester Quadra-Jet, and slightly higher lift camshaft.

For the serious enthusiast, the big block was the engine of choice, and Chevrolet offered four different Turbo Jet 396 rat motors. The standard 396, which could be ordered only with the SS, was the 325-horsepower L35 package. Next step was the L34 350 horsepower 396, followed by a pair of asphalt-melting, solid lifter monsters, the L78 and the L89. The L78 featured iron heads, big Holly carburetor, and special free-flow exhausts that looked a lot like cast iron headers. The L89 boasted the same except it featured aluminum heads and weighed significantly less than the iron head L78. Both were conservatively rated at 375 horsepower (although their output was more like 425 to 450 horsepower) to prevent the insurance companies from slapping additional surcharges on the already high premiums young enthusiast drivers were paying.

One of the sweetest options offered on the SS package was the chambered exhaust (RPO NC8). Specially tuned for minimum back flow, the chambered exhaust had a lovely "rumpity-rump" basso pro-

1969 Camaro — See How They Ran						
RPO	HP	Carb	Trans	0–60	Quarter Mile	Magazine
LM1	255	QJ	THM	9.6	17.5/83.0	*SCG* 10/68
L48	300	QJ	4M	8.3	15.9/88.0	*MT* 3/69
L78	375	H	4M	6.8	14.77/98.72	*CL* 5/69

SCG = Sports Car Graphic   MT = Motor Trend   CL = Car Life

Notice blacked out grille on this RS/SS and slits over headlamp doors, to permit light to come through if the doors failed to open.

fundo sound and was the deal of the year at $15.80. Unfortunately, it was ordered by only 1,526 buyers.

The 1969 Camaro went on sale September 26, 1968, and was an immediate hit. Buyers responded to the new aggressive styling at a time when industry sales as a whole were down 9.3 percent and the ponycar segment contracted by 100,000 units. The Camaro's sales performance mirrored this downturn, accounting for 7.9 percent of Chevrolet total sales in 1969.

The L48 was standard with the SS350 package. It was rated at 300 horsepower.

1969 Performance Engine Production

RPO	CID	HP	Production
L65	350	250	26,898
L48	350	300	22,339
L34	396	350	2,018
L35	396	325	6,752
L78	396	375	4,889
L89	396	375	311

The 1969 Camaro was due for a long production run since the next generation F-car wouldn't be ready until early 1970. First introduced with the rest of the 1969 Chevrolet product lineup on September 26, 1968, it was still around when the 1970 cars were introduced on September 18, 1969. About the only change made was to the VIN plate to reflect the car was sold as a 1970 model instead of a 1969.

Total Camaro sales for the 1969 model year amounted to 159,202. This pales next to the sales success of 1967–1968; however, the buying

Big thumpin' 375-horsepower L78 could be had with aluminum heads as well (RPO L89). Like most solid lifter engines, it needed constant tuning to run properly.

1969 Camaro Performance Engines

RPO	CID/HP	Torque	Compression
L34	396/350 @ 5200	415 @ 3400	10.25:1
L35	396/325 @ 4800	410 @ 3200	10.25:1
L78	396/375 @ 5600	415 @ 3600	11.0:1
L89	396/375 @ 5600	415 @ 3600	11.0:1*
L65	350/250 @ 4800	345 @ 2800	9.0:1
L48	350/300 @ 4800	380 @ 3200	10.25:1

* Aluminum head (74 lb. weight savings over L78 iron head)

public had been reading numerous articles about the next-generation Camaro and many chose to wait until the new 1970 $^1/_2$ models appeared. Chevrolet kept the 1969 Camaro in the product lineup as long as dealers could continue to put them over the curb. From the September 18, 1969 introduction to February 26, 1970, the Camaro sold an additional 83,883 units for a total production run of 243,085.

Percentage of Factory Installed Equipment— 1969 Camaro

Automatic transmission	60.6
Four-speed transmission	27.3
V8 Engine	73.2
Six-cylinder engine	26.7
AM radio	84.9
Air conditioning	18.4
Tilt column	2.7
Power steering	49.3
Power drum brakes	34.0
Power disc brakes	27.6
Power windows	1.1
Vinyl top	41.3
Tinted windshield	1.1
Tinted windows/windshield	47.1
Limited slip differential	20.0
Wheel covers	46.3
Speed regulating device	0.08

At the Drags

The Super Stock and Stock classes tightened up in 1969. Dodge and Plymouth dominated Super Stock, although Malcolm Durham grabbed a 10.60 ET in his 1969 Camaro for AHRA Super Stock Eliminator. In the NHRA, Glen Self snared the F/MP class with his 1969 Camaro, turning 12.68/80.21, making it to Street Eliminator, and taking the trophy run with a 12.35/109.89.

RS/SS350 coupe in Madeira Maroon with UPC P12 wheels (included with SS package) and UPC 308 black vinyl top.

RS/SS396 in Nantucket Blue with Custom interior and P12 wheels

How much Camaro you want depends on how much driver you want to be.

Top:
Camaro-about-town. The sport coupe. Buckets. Carpeting. Fully synchronized 3-speed. Very civilized Six. Safety features like dual master cylinder brake system with warning light. Especially nice for wife-types.

Center:
Country-club Camaro. Rally Sport with hideaway headlights and standard V8, 210 hp. Add custom interior, Powerglide, console, wheel covers, vinyl roof cover, stereo tape system. Decorate right front seat suitably.

Bottom:
Camaro the Magnificent. SS convertible, now available with 396 cu. in., 325 hp! Bulging hood, striped nose, red stripe tires all come. You order the 4-speed, front disc brakes, Positraction and such. At your Chevrolet dealer's.

Command Performance
CHEVROLET
Camaro

GM
MARK OF EXCELLENCE

Chevrolet chose "Command Performance" as the theme for the 1967 Camaro advertising campaign. It was important that the Camaro establish an image as quickly as possible to make a substantial dent in Mustang sales. This ad introduced the three different Camaro models and established their separate identities.

Smile when you call it Detroit iron

Oh, sure, Camaro is comfortable as all get-out and the heater works. But that doesn't mean it's a motorized marshmallow. It's a real driving machine without the old-fashioned sports car symptoms of chilblains, sore bones and sharp shooting pains in the wallet.

Camaro will make a believer out of you if you don't think so. It has what it takes, including engines up to an exclusive new 350-cubic-inch V8 you can order, handling that's just as *pur sang* as you could want, front disc brakes available and all the other earmarks of a real driving machine.

It has safety in mind, too, with items like GM-developed energy-absorbing steering column, safety door latches and hinges, padded instrument panel and back-up lights standard.

So smile, call it Detroit iron, enjoy the foam cushioning and quiet running, and go show those purists.

Camaro SS 350 Convertible with Rally Sport equipment.

Command Performance

Camaro by CHEVROLET

CAMARO SS 350—The accent's on fun in this one with special suspension, new 350-cubic-inch V8, big red stripe tires on 14 x 6-inch rims, 2¼-inch dual exhausts, all standard. It looks the part, too, with a special striping and louver-styled hood, plus special identification emblems.

CAMARO RALLY SPORT—Change the appearance of Camaro by ordering the Rally Sport package. It has hidden headlights in a full-width black grille, special taillight treatment and special exterior trim. You can order the SS 350 and Rally Sport packages together, too, for double the pleasure.

Dramatic shot of the RS/SS350's grille and long hood emphasized power. Instrument panel with optional in-dash tachometer and console mounted gauge package is shown in inset.

To meet Federal emissions standards, an Air Injection Reactor (A.I.R.) pump was plumbed into the engine's emission system. The A.I.R. robbed power, and it often was the first thing customers tossed when they took delivery.

SS396 in Garnet Red. Notice hood with dummy air inlets.

Standard interior
with optional con-
sole and console
mounted gauge
cluster.

SS350 in Hugger Orange with
N66 Sport Wheels. Vinyl tops
were popular on Camaros in
1969; over 43,000 were installed.

Pace cars were loaded with options. This one boasts air conditioning, gauges, AM/FM radio, wood accents and full gauge package.

Penske Racing team struggled during the 1967 Trans-Am season as they learned to dial in the cars, but did manage to win the last two races. This was the lightweight car built just during the 1967 season.

Note paint stripe on ducktail spoiler. Factory-painted stripes did not cover the trailing edge of the decklid.

Z/28 engine compartment showing aluminum high-rise intake manifold and log style exhaust manifolds.

Daytona Yellow Z/28 with RS package. Note 302 emblem on ZL2 hood. Rally Sport nameplate remains on front fender behind wheel opening and Z/28 badge is located in left side of grille.

Yenko Super Camaro for 1969 in Hugger Orange. Yenko used stock hood in 1969, customized interior and exterior with stripes and decals.

Chevrolet drag racers loved the Camaro for its big engines and light weight. This Camaro "funny car," the Dixie Twister, was actually a fiberglass body on a welded tubular frame. Here driver Huston Platt sticks it to Tasca Ford's Single Overhead Camshaft 427.

RS/SS350 with White Houndstooth interior and N34 Sports Styled steering wheel with wood grained rim and ZJ7 Rally Wheels. RPO D90 Sport Striping was standard as part of the SS package. Aside from VIN changes, the 1969 Camaro was carried over unchanged as a 1970 model. The 1970 1/2 proportions Camaros were released on February 26, 1970.

1969 Camaro Indy Pace Car

For the second time in three years, a Camaro SS396 convertible paced the 53rd Indianapolis 500 on May 30, 1969. Two identical cars, with the exception of the tires (one was equipped with Firestones, the other with Goodyears), performed the actual pace duties, driven by former Indy 500 winner and Chevrolet dealer Jim Rathmann. The race winner, Mario Andretti, received the third pace car, this time equipped with air conditioning and power top.

Chevrolet provided 133 1969 Camaros as festival pace cars. The Indy Committee received 43 cars, 75 were designated for VIP use, and 7 were for Speedway use. USAC officials used 5 cars. Two paced the race, and the race winner received the third.

Because of the popularity of the Indy pace cars, Chevrolet chose to build a limited run of replicas for sale to the public. The convertible replicas were designated RPO Z11, and 3,675 copies were built. The Z11 started as a Dover White Camaro SS/RS and was then modified to include Hugger Orange paint stripes, the body sill was painted white instead of black, and the rear panel was painted white instead of black as specified with 396 engine options. The RPO D90 Sport Striping option was stripped off and Hugger Orange fender stripping was installed instead. The Custom Interior featured Orange houndstooth cloth trim. The new ZL2 air induction hood and 15-inch Rally wheels were installed.

Pace car replicas weren't all convertibles. Approximately 200 RPO Z10 Pace Car hardtops were also built at the Norwood plant from late April to mid May as a regional promotion and sold through dealers in the upper Midwest. Chevrolet also promoted a "Pacesetter Value Package" that included the 350 engine, power front disc brakes, and deluxe wheel covers—this saved $147 over the separate purchase of these options.

Most of the Z10 and Z11 replicas were equipped with the following options, though other options and packages also could be ordered:

50-50	Color—Dover White	YA1	Custom Deluxe seat belts
720BA	Interior—Orange Houndstooth	ZL2	Special Ducted Hood (cowl induction)
Z27	Camaro SS Option	D80	Rear spoiler
Z87	Custom Interior	ZJ7	Rally wheels
Z22	Rally Sport Option	Z11	Indy Pace Car Package

These options were incorporated into the actual pace cars along with the following:

M40	Turbo Hydra-Matic	U17	Special instrumentation
G80	Positraction rear	U63	AM pushbutton radio
N40	Power steering	D80	Air spoiler equipment
C06	Power convertible top	N34	Sport styled steering wheel
D55	Center console	A01	Soft Ray tinted glass
YA1	Custom Deluxe seat and front shoulder belts (A39 &A85)		

Left: The Indy Pace Car Package was RPO Z11, The "Super Scoop" ZL2 hood was part of the package. Pace cars were painted Dover White with orange stripes.

Below: RS/SS396 pace car had no problem leading the Indycars at speeds up to 120 mph. Chevrolet dealer and former Indy 500 winner Jim Rathmann drove the pacecar.

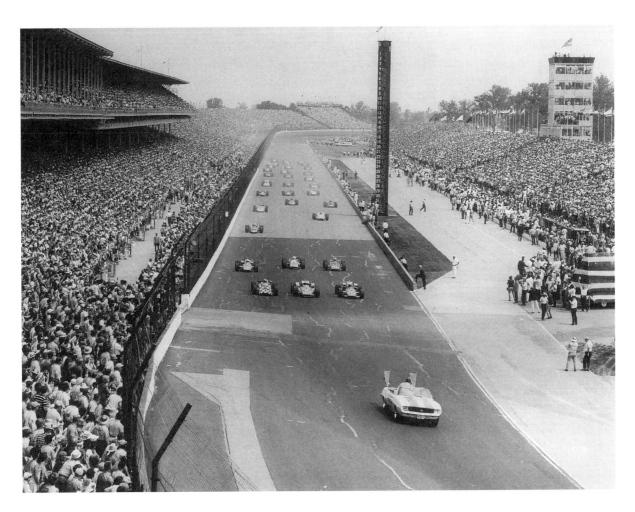

Trim tag on cowl shows Z11
code to authenticate Pace
Car coupe.

The RPO Z10 Indy Pace Car
hardtop package was marketed in the Mid-West prior to
the race. About 200 were
sold. Dressed out just like the
Z11 convertible, the Z10
coupe sported the same
Dover White paint, orange
paint stripes and orange
houndstooth interior. No
Pace Car coupes were used
at the Indy race.

Above: The tail lamp panel was not blacked out on pace cars, even though they were RS/SS models.

Left: Standard 300-horsepower SS350 engine was installed in some of the pace car replicas.

Chevrolet proudly advertised the selection of the Camaro for the Indy 500 pace duties. A special "Pacesetter Value Package" was offered nationally that included 350 engine, power front disc brakes and deluxe wheel covers. Chevrolet provided 133 RS/SS Camaros as festival cars for the Indianapolis 500 race.

The 1969 Camaro SS keeps tough company.

For two out of the last three years it's been chosen the official Indy 500 pace car. Check one out and you'll know why.

Engine choices start with a 300-hp 350 V8 and work their way up. For more power, a special new intake hood is available. We call it Super Scoop. It opens on acceleration, ramming huge gulps of air to the engine.

Additional credentials: beefed-up suspension, white-lettered wide ovals on 14" x 7" wheels, power disc brakes and a special transmission with floor shift.

It takes a lot to get this crowd started. That's why Camaro SS sets the pace.

For competition to follow.

CHEVROLET

Putting you first, keeps us first.

Camaro SS...and friends.

Camaro SS Convertible with Rally Sport equipment and new Super Scoop.

Compared to the rest of the ponycar segment, the Camaro captured 22.5 percent of the market in 1969. That sales performance was more than satisfactory and was indicative of the strength the Camaro nameplate had in the marketplace. "For us at Chevrolet, it was an exciting program," Alex Mair reminisced. "We had all these fun things going on like the pace cars, the Trans-Am racing and having all these performance models like the SS350 and the SS396."

Although GM came to market late in the game after Ford had hit a homerun with the Mustang, in three short years the Camaro had wrestled a significant part of the market away from Ford's ponycar. Considering the reluctance within some GM quarters to even build the car and then the mad rush to get it through development with numerous compromises, the first-generation Camaro was remarkable in proving itself to be a profitable addition to the Chevrolet lineup.

Vince Piggins was head of Chevrolet Product
Promotions and the father of the Z/28.

Chapter Five

Z/28—The Instant Legend

1967

> *"A ho-hum Camaro started down the road in '66 and reached a fork where the sign pointing left read 'race cars' and the one to the right read, 'sporty cars.' Restrained by corporate policy from fielding a works team in the Trans-Am series, Chevrolet took both roads anyway."*
> — Sports Car Graphic

The job of putting together a "race car" Camaro program to beat Mustang went to Vince Piggins, head of Chevrolet Product Promotions. Within Detroit's superheated competitive environment, the timing and the venue couldn't have been better. The SCCA had provided the venue with its new "Trans-Am" Group 2 sedan racing series. Although Chrysler-backed Bob Tulius in his Dodge Dart competed early on, it was Piggins and his crosstown competitors at Ford that knew it wouldn't take long for the Trans-Am to heat up into a classic Chevy versus Ford battle. "We had reasons to believe," recalled Paul King, "that the Camaro would be very competitive in that series, and that sales advantage would be worth the cost of development."

Ford jumped in first with a back-door team of two Mustangs assembled by Shelby-American. Ford also funded a Cougar effort headed by Parnelli Jones and Dan Gurney. With that kind of head start, it was no surprise that the Mustang and Cougar teams shared 8 out of 11 victories in the 1966 series.

Put all the parts together and you have a high winding 302 cubic inch screamer rated at 290 horsepower. The Z/28's iron heads boasted big 2.02-inch intake and 1.60-inch exhaust valves. With the big ports and large passages, the Z/28's iron heads could move a lot of air.

Piggins saw the *Wham! Slam!* Trans-Am racing as the perfect venue to prove the Camaro's superiority over the Mustang and Cougar. Even before the new Camaro was released to the public in September 1966, Piggins was savvy enough to make sure SCCA officials knew Chevrolet's intentions to race and helped define the series specifications. He was also able to make a commitment to support the teams that raced the Camaro with engineering and parts assistance, even though "Chevrolet did not participate in racing."

First, Piggins had to homologate an engine that came in under the Trans-Am displacement limit of 305 cubic inches. Chevrolet offered the 283 and the 327 in their engine lineup, but nothing in between. The 283 wasn't stout enough and the 327 was too large, but Piggins deduced that mating the four-inch bore of the 327 with the three-inch stroke of the 283 provided a displacement of 302.4 cubic inches. This was a tried and true combination that racers had used before, and it met

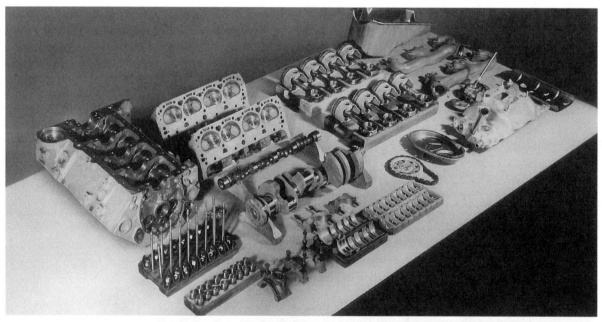

The 302 was born from the mating of the 283 engine's crank with the 327 engine's bore. Log style exhaust manifolds were standard. Headers were optional equipment.

A Small-Block Screamer in a Big-Block World

Corvette owners had been debating the merits of big-block versus small-block power for several years when the Z/28 appeared. Of course, Chevrolet was mandated by the SCCA displacement cap of 305 cubic inches for the Z/28, but in bringing this engine to the street, it taught a lot of bow tie fans that displacement wasn't always the replacement for horsepower. Not only was the high revving 302 fun to drive, it also missed the insurance premium surcharge penalty extended to all large displacement engines.

---

the SCCA's legal 305-cubic inch ceiling. It also meant that the 302 would inherit the intrinsic benefits of having a short stroke with an oversquare bore. A short-stroke engine can run at higher rpms for longer periods since there is less piston speed. That, of course, is what a race engine has to do—run for sustained durations at high rpms.

The small-journal, cast iron block for the 302 was also shared with the 327 and the 350 engines in 1967. The crankshafts were forged steel and tuftrided for high rpm durability. The rods were shot peened and mated to 11.0:1 domed aluminum pistons with notched valve relieves. The iron heads featured big 2.02″ intake and 1.60″ exhaust valves with

What made the 302 go like stink was the superb combination of big bore block, short stroke crank, forged rods with high compression pistons, big-valve heads and the optional Cross Ram dual carburetor and big tube headers.

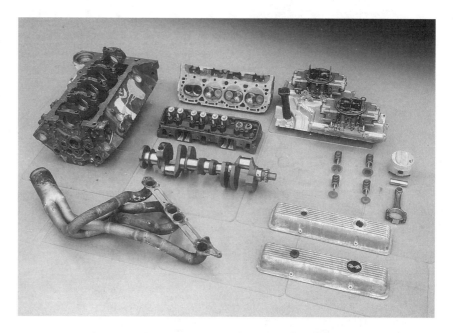

wide passages and generous ports, again to pronounce mid and high-end horsepower response. The 302's "30/30" camshaft was lifted from the 375-horsepower Corvette 327 fuelie engine and designed for use with solid lifters.

A big 800-cfm, dual-pumper Holley carburetor was bolted to a tuned-runner, dual plane aluminum intake manifold with the front crossover tapped for a temperature sensor. Log-style iron exhaust manifolds were standard with headers optional. A single point Delco-Remy ignition was standard with a transistorized ignition optional. Chevrolet blatantly underrated the 302's horsepower at 290 and torque at an equally silly 290 lb-ft. In reality, the production engines generated over 375 horsepower, with power coming on strong from 3500 to 6500 rpm and still pulling at 7000 rpm.

Piggins' concept of using off-the-shelf, high-performance componentry to build both a spirited performance street engine and a wicked race engine had another advantage. He could come to market with a production engine using off-the-shelf parts at significant cost savings. That would make it easier to sell the program to Chevrolet management.

Chevrolet Engineering and Product Planning assembled the rest of the package, which Piggins referred to as "The Cheetah." Air conditioning and automatic transmission were not offered. Due to body rigidity problems, Engineering decided against a convertible version. The 302 was to be mated to a four-speed Muncie manual gearbox, heavy-duty F41 suspension, power-assisted front disc brakes with sintered metallic drums in the rear, fast ratio steering, and a cold air induction plenum.

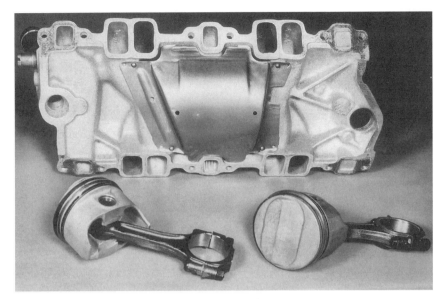

Aluminum high-rise intake was specially designed for the Z/28. Windage tray was not used in production engines. "Pink" rods were shot-peened and mated to 11.0:1 forged aluminum pistons. Holley double pumper was rated at 800cfm.

Piggins took Chevrolet General Manager Pete Estes for a demonstration drive in October 1966 at General Motor's Milford Proving Grounds outside Detroit. Piggins was a capable performance driver and it didn't take him long to convince Estes to approve the project. "Estes was the driving force behind the Z/28," remembers Chief Engineer Alex Mair. In fact, Estes was actually the unsung hero behind many of the great performance cars that came from both Pontiac and Chevrolet in the 1960s including the Pontiac GTO.

On the dyno, the cross ram added twenty-five horsepower to the 302's advertised rating of 290. Real power output of the 302 was more in the area of 350-375 horsepower.

Tagged as the next RPO after the Z27 SS Camaro Super Sport Option Package, the 302 Special Performance Equipment Option was designated Z/28, which was quickly accepted as the model name for this new race-oriented Camaro. The Z/28 was released to the press for first driving impressions at Riverside Raceway in November 1966. Chevrolet hyped the new Camaro by saying "The Z/28 package was developed to make the Camaro an exceptional touring machine having relatively light weight, a smaller but highly responsive V8 engine with four-speed transmission and suspension refinements that result in excellent stability and handling characteristics." Available, but not part of the Z/28 package, was a rear deck spoiler developed by Chevrolet Research & Development Engineer Paul Van Valkenburg and styled by Larry Shinoda.

The base Z/28 package cost $328.10 and included the 302-cubic inch engine, 3.73.1 rear axle, dual exhausts, and 15 x 6 stamped steel wheels on 7.35 x 14 nylon red line tires. Heavy-duty suspension, heavy-duty radiator, and special wide stripes were also part of the package. There were three additional Z/28 option packages, all built on the base option. The Z/282 option cost $437.10 and included all of the Z/28 package plus a cowl induction plenum/air cleaner assembly delivered

Standard 1967 interior featured nylon loop carpeting, vinyl padded door panels and bow tie emblem in horn button of standard three-spoke steering wheel.

This black Custom interior has optional center console with gauge package and 7,000 rpm in-dash tachometer.

Standard Red interior with optional console. Two-spoke steering wheel was standard, featured horn tabs in each spoke. Upholstery was all vinyl.

Early publicity shot of 1967 Z/28 with Rally Sport package and optional D80 duck-tail spoiler.

P-12 Special wheel trim was standard with front wheel disc brakes. Tires were 7.35 x 14.

Z/282 option included the base Z/28 package plus the cowl induction plenum/air cleaner assembly. These components were shipped from the factory for installation by the dealer or the customer. The plenum went through several designs during 1967 production run.

loose in the trunk to be installed by the dealer. The Z/283 package cost $779.40 and added a set of exhaust headers delivered loose in the trunk for dealer installation. The Z/284 package included all of the above packages for a cost of $858.40. A four-speed manual gearbox was a mandatory option and was available in close- or wide-ratio configurations. Another mandatory option was power-assisted front disc brakes with rear drum brakes.

Production of the 1967 Z/28 ramped up slowly, beginning on December 29, 1966. A handful of cars were delivered in early January to dealers like Yenko, Nickey, and Dana for preparation to race in the Trans-Am sedan series and other venues. These first cars were built for racers—no radio, heater, or body sound deadener—and not intended for the general public. Many of the 602 Z/28s built in 1967 also included the Rally Sport option, although it was not mandatory. Chevrolet was supposed to produce 1,000 Z/28s to meet SCCA/FIA homologation rules; however, Chevrolet found a way around that by homologating the SS350 under FIA Group 1 rules, then qualifying the Z/28 option under Group 2 rules. One of the reasons only 602 Z/28s were sold was a complete lack of marketing support on the part of Chevrolet. Many dealers had no idea what a Z/28 was, and it was not pushed by the zone sales managers. Those who wanted to go sedan racing knew what Z/28 stood for and found a dealer who would order one.

1967 Z/28 with Rally Sport package. Note absence of Z/28 emblems. It wasn't until 1968 that Z/28s wore nameplates on the front fenders.

In 1967, front header panel and rear deck emblems had Chevrolet script with Camaro nameplate below.

1967 Z/28 in base package. Note absence of bright metal trim at wheel openings, roof drip rails and no engine emblems. Remove the black stripes and no one would know it was a Z/28 — until the engine was started.

Only 602 Z/28s were built in 1967, way below the 1000 minimum required by SCCA for Group 2 homologation. Chevorlet found a loophole that allowed homologation of the SS350 package under Group 1 rules and then qualifying the Z/28 option under Group 2 rules.

Early production Z/28s wore 302 badges on front fenders. Fifteen-inch ZJ7 Rally wheels were part of Z/28 package and featured a new center cap.

The Z/28 package was an enormous improvement to the Camaro; however, cornering and braking agility was still dampened by its Achilles heel—the monoplate leaf rear suspension. *Car and Driver* noted that under heavy acceleration, "reaction to the engine's torque tips the car counterclockwise, unloading the right rear wheel. If the right side of the axle isn't tied down, it goes haywire." *Car and Driver* also noted "under heavy braking, the torque is coming from the opposite direction and the left side of the axle judders violently."

What's important to remember about the Z/28 was how unique its mission was. While the rest of the Camaro lineup was designed and built around the standard parameters for street cars (a trait *Car and Driver* referred to as "a polished lack of character"), the Z/28 had been produced to homologate a race car package. The parts selected for the package fell within higher specifications not usually used by Detroit carmakers. By doing so, Chevrolet—unwittingly or not—came close to building one of the best American sports sedans ever made. "With the Z/28," *Car and Driver* observed, "Chevy is on the way toward making the gutsy stormer the Camaro should have been in the first place."

Jerry Titus, editor of *Sports Car Graphic* and a competent race driver himself, summed it best when he observed, "Where the Z/28 is significant is in the breakthrough of the stubborn policy to hold back options and hardware that would enable customers to be more competitive."

Titus knew that Chevrolet wouldn't provide factory-racing support. "It looks like Camaro competitors may have to depend on prize money

Z/28 iin base trim package and front bumper guards.

for support," Titus wrote in *Sports Car Graphic* in March 1967, "Yet the vehicle itself will give them a fair shot at it and that, after all, is the name of the game."

Chevrolet was anxious to get the Z/28 on the track against the Mustang. Piggins had already arranged with Roger Penske to build a two-car team. Penske had a long relationship with Chevrolet, racing Corvettes at Daytona and Sebring and Chevy-powered Lolas in the Cam Am series. Penske put together a team with Mark Donohue to do the development and driving duties. George Wintersteen picked up one of the first-production Z/28s at the Norwood assembly plant and drove it to Penske's facility near Philadelphia. The red with black stripes Z/28 had no radio, heater, or body insulation. Donohue and mechanic Bill Mayberry began tearing it down while Traco put together the engine.

Donohue had difficulty dialing in the Camaro's suspension and braking needs, and after four races Piggins reluctantly realized that

Donohue needed help in finding the handle. Piggins and Corvette engineers like Gib Hufstader and Dick Rider attacked the problems of brakes and suspension, even to the point of bringing the car to GM's Milford Proving Grounds for a covert battery of tests that included aerodynamics, spring combinations, and more brake work. It was obvious to Piggins and Chevrolet management that their help was essential if the Z/28 was going to accomplish its goal of beating the factory-backed Mustangs and winning the Trans-Am series.

By the end of the season, Chevrolet engineers like Jim Musser had found the right combinations and Donohue began to win races. Penske built a second car, a lighter weight version that boasted acid-dipped body panels. While that car was under construction, their first car was heavily damaged in an accident while being transported to California. The lightweight car had to be hurried to completion. Although it made it to the Modesto race, an incorrect rear axle gear stymied the car's performance.

The first car was rebuilt and campaigned along with the lightweight car; however, Chevrolet's resolve to continue supplying Donohue with engineering assistance and parts was beginning to wane. The Ford and Cougar teams were wailing on Chevrolet, and there was little Chrysler could do to remain competitive. As Chevrolet Research and Development Engineer Paul Van Valkenburg related in *Chevrolet—*

Chevrolet didn't spend time and money helping Mark Donohue to correct the Camaro's inherent cornering and brake faults without some payback. That came in the form of electronic data gathered during testing at Milford and at several races where Chevrolet engineers appeared incognito.

Along with applying some of the knowledge learned to improving production Camaros, Chevrolet Engineering had built a test car using tricks learned from the Penske racecar. As Paul Van Valkenburg recalls in *Chevrolet—Racing*, "Its suspension was much stiffer than production, and at various times it ran with dozens of different combinations of springs, shocks, anti-roll bars, optional geometry and competition tires."

Perhaps the most significant spin-off to this research was the construction and testing of an independent rear suspension for the Camaro. Testing showed that in most cases the independent rear suspension borrowed from the Corvette barely outperformed the standard leaf spring rear suspension. Ultimately it was found to be too expensive to tool for the Camaro and was dropped.

Restored Penske/Godshall 1967 Z/28 Trans-Am racecar powers out of the corner during recent nostalgia sports car race.

Racing, "Politics and personalities were clashing behind the scenes at Chevrolet. Management was upset about the Camaro/Mustang showing in the Trans-Am, and the engineers were explaining that they couldn't solve the problems by telepathy." Since Chevrolet prohibited overt factory support, engineers couldn't have a high profile at the races. "All their sophisticated tools and instrumentation," Van Valkenburg wrote, "would be too obvious at any race track and no one wanted to be responsible for allowing Penske's cars on GM facilities."

Fortunately, Piggins and Chevrolet Engineering hung in with Donohue, finding ways to covertly appear at tracks and provide assistance. As the season drew to a close, the results began to pay off. The suspension was now dialed in and responsive, the severe brake fading was solved, and the TRACO 302 engine was delivering 420 reliable horsepower. The Penske Camaros won the last two events of the 1967 Trans-Am season at Las Vegas and Kent. As the season ended, the record showed Chrysler with one win, Ford and Cougar scoring four victories each, and Camaro with two.

Smokey Yunick was back at Sebring in 1968 with his mystery Z/28 driven by Al Unser and Lloyd Ruby. The engine blew on lap 43 and the team was done for the day. *Walt Thurn photo*

The Best Damn Rule Bender in Town

Roger Penske wasn't the only racer to bring the Camaro into competition. At most races, there were as many Camaros as Mustangs. However, aside from Penske, they were in the hands of privateers and ran at the back of the pack, if they finished at all. Legendary mechanic Smokey Yunick, who field-tested many of the components that Chevrolet Research & Development developed for the Z/28, entered his "interpretation" of a Trans-Am Group 2 sedan. Yunick's Camaro was narrowed, channeled, chopped, and dropped. The body seams were filled, the windows were flushed, and the car was just plain illegal. During tech inspection, SCCA officials directed Yunick to tear virtually half the car down for inspection, including dropping the fuel tank. When advised there were seven changes that had to be made to make the car legal, Yunick said "Might as well make that eight" and drove off, leaving the fuel tank laying in the garage at the tech inspector's feet.

Yunick had also built a Trans-Am Camaro that looked to outperform the Penske entry at Sebring, but, in characteristic style, he and the SCCA soon parted ways. In October 1967, he took his specially prepared black and gold Z/28 to Bonneville and went hunting for world speed records. Yunick and three drivers—Curtis Tuner, Mickey Thompson, and Bunkie Blackburn—hit the salts in a USAC/FIA-sanctioned attempt that broke or set 259 new records. Yunick's Camaro recorded a top speed of 174 mph with a 302 engine. He then dropped a big block between those narrowed fenders and clicked off a top speed of 183 mph.

1968

While there were few exterior changes to the 1968 Z/28, considerable alterations were made under the sheet metal. Early production 1968 Z/28s received 302 badges on the fenders. In March 1968, Chevrolet chose to promote and market the Z/28 as a separate model, so Z/28 emblems replaced the 302 fender badges. While not part of the Z/28 package, the D80 fiberglass rear ducktail spoiler and chin spoiler (known officially as the "Auxiliary Panel and Valance") was offered. The Z/28 also received all modifications and upgrades made to 1968 Camaro models, especially the switch to a multileaf rear suspension for V8 cars. Tire size was upgraded to E70 x 15 2 ply (4-ply rating).

Refinements were made to the 302 engine for 1968. Some of these upgrades came at the beginning of the production year, while others were rolled in production during midyear. The 302 block was still shared with the 327 and the 350 engines; however, it now boasted larger journals and a large journal crankshaft (2.10-inch rod journals and 2.449-inch main journals). First production rods featured pressed pins and larger rod bolts, while second production rods were changed to floating wrist pins. Pistons were also changed in midyear. First production 302 pistons were similar to 1967 units, however the domes were notched across the entire head of the piston. Cylinder heads and camshaft usage remained unchanged.

In March 1968, the Z/28 badge replaced the 302 emblem on the front fender.

The Z/28 package was still not designed for the mild-mannered driver. "It is noisy," noted *Car Life*, "almost scary in its response to all controls and delivers a steady barrage of soft blows to the hindsides of its occupants." *Car Life* also observed, "This Camaro needs to be driven, in every sense of the word. To the man capable of extracting them the Z/28 has a storeroom of treasures. For enjoyment per dollar, the Z/28 must be one of the bargains of the decade."

What the high-winding 302 lacked in low-end torque was made up in thrilling mid- and top-end acceleration. "Above 30 mph," *Car Life* noted, "on winding mountain roadways, back country lanes and the rest of the types of roads which make driving worth doing, the Z/28 Camaro is an exhilarating vehicle. The Z/28 engine is a jewel, an outstanding performer by any yardstick."

What had bow tie fans excited was the $500 cross ram package homologated for Trans-Am competition and offered over the counter for the Z/28. The cross ram had first been conceived in 1966 for use with the big block with conversion to small-block application taking place in the summer of 1967. Actually intended more for race use, customers could purchase and install the cross ram for street use themselves or have the dealer install it for them. Good for at least an addi-

Close-up of Cross Ram engineering prototype. Note absence of chokes. Two-piece ram log runners were just over 13 inches in length.

Estes' special order Z/28 Camaro convertible was equipped with prototype ZL2 hood, Cross ram package and headers. Note hood pins and outside remote control mirror.

It's Good to Be the Boss

Production records show that no Z/28 convertibles were ever built. As is always the case, one should "never say never." Chevrolet General Manager Pete Estes managed a little pull at Chevrolet and arranged for a Z/28 ragtop to be built for him. It is the only one known to exist.

tional 25 horsepower, the cross ram started with a special, dual-quad aluminum intake manifold with tuned runners and featured a pair of Holley 600-cfm double pumpers. The cross ram lacked manifold heat crossovers or chokes for the carburetors and was difficult to drive on the street. Its true purpose was on the racetrack, where it could pull more horsepower out of the high-winding 302.

The cross ram used a cowl induction air cleaner and plenum to take advantage of the cooler, high-pressure air located at the base of the windshield. This cool air provided a denser charge and more power. While it was great on the racetrack, most testers found it impractical for

The Penske Racing team dominated the 1968 Trans-Am season, winning 10 out of the 13 races and running away with the Manufacturer's Championship. Not only was Donohue and the #6 Z/28 invincible, but the Penske pit crew was the best in the business.

street use. "If the Z/28 isn't a bona fide racing car—in street clothing—then we've never seen one," observed *Road & Track*. The cross ram was available over the counter in December 1967, in time for Chevrolet to homologate it for 1968 SCCA competition.

Product planning chose to eliminate the Z/282, Z/283, and Z/284 package options before the end of the 1968 production run since few customers were willing to pay the extra costs, including the ridiculously high sticker price for the headers.

Thanks to the research and data collected with Donohue's race car, Chevrolet engineers developed a four-wheel disc package that became available in March 1968 as a "Heavy-Duty Service Package" to conform to SCCA/FIA rules. Though this over-the-counter service option was primarily geared for racers, it was suitable for dealer or customer installation.

Racing

Coming off the successes of the last two races of the season, it seemed a given that Penske Racing would be in the thick of the 1968 battle. Along with updating the lightweight car, the team built a new 1968 race car for the major races, adding lightweight pieces. Engine problems, including a cracked head, held the car back in the Daytona 24, resulting in a less than spectacular second in class, 64 laps behind the Mustang of Titus/Bucknam.

Pit stops had also been a serious problem at Daytona, with the Penske crew taking too long to remove and replace the calipers. Bill Howell from Chevrolet Engineering developed a method of using vacuum to hold the brake pistons in place, allowing the calipers to be removed and replaced much faster. Instead of four minutes to change pads, Howell got it down to one minute forty seconds. That advantage gave Camaro at least a one additional lap lead when the Mustangs pitted for new brakes.

At Sebring, the two Penske Camaros dominated the race, winning first and second in the GT class and third and fourth overall (Porsche took first and second overall). The Ford efforts finished no higher than twelfth overall. Ford was finding out the TRACO 302 engine was more than capable of trouncing their new Tunnel-Port 302 engine on the long courses.

The rest of the 1968 season was a series of disappointments for the Mustang teams. Mechanical failures, blown engines, and freaky accidents conspired to drop the Ford teams out of the running for the next eight races after Sebring. The Penske team secured the Trans-Am championship at the Bryar race with 105 points to Ford's 63. The final results were ten wins for Camaro, three wins for Ford.

During the 1968 season, the Penske crew was invited to bring their Camaro back to Detroit for a vehicle dynamics analysis by Chevrolet Engineering. Chevrolet was in the process of writing a manual on how to build a Camaro racecar (*Camaro Chassis Preparation*) for privateers, and the work done by Chevrolet engineers and Mark Donohue was the foundation for the material. While the race car was at Milford, Chevrolet Engineering gathered new data on spoiler position and angles for application on the 1969 cars.

On the grid at Sebring, March 1968. The Penske team was famous for attention to detail in preparing their racecars. The #15 car qualified first, finished third overall and first in class driven by Donohue and Fisher.

Traco-built 440-horsepower 302 race engine in Mark Donohue's Z/28 at Sebring, March 1968. Note cross ram and cowl induction.

The Real Numbers?

According to Chevrolet, the 302 produced 290 horsepower @ 5800 rpm and 290 lb-ft of torque @ 4200 rpm. There's no question the 302 was underrated, but by how much? Insiders talk about 375 horsepower at 6800 rpm. Road testers could take the 302 to beyond 7000 rpm and the engine was still pulling. Keeping the horsepower rating low kept the insurance premiums down for youthful drivers and was a transparent foil for SCCA specifications.

For Penske, his TRACO-built competition engines produced an easy 420 horsepower and could push 450 with a seasoned block and fresh heads. It was this power, combined with incredible durability, that made the Z/28 so competitive in the Trans-Am series.

Z/28 Production—1967–1969

Year	Production
1967	602
1968	7,199
1969	20,302

1969

The Z/28 truly came into its own in 1969. "News of Roger and Mark's Trans-Am expedition has finally reached the Chevrolet marketing minions," noted *Sports Car Graphic*, "and they've caught the fever." After two years of racing and dozens of magazine road tests, Chevrolet marketing was finally getting behind the Z/28 and carrying the word from Detroit to dealers nationwide. The Z/28 went through a transition, becoming a balanced street performance car rather than an uncivilized brute wearing painted suspenders.

When it came to the 302 engine, Chevrolet was not without its detractors. The complaints didn't stem from the engine's innate ability to wind to high rpms. Instead, questions rose about the 302's merits as a street performance engine. Corvette Chief Engineer Zora Arkus Duntov called the 302 "an artificial engine built to meet an artificial class limit." Within the context of Trans-Am racing, the 302 had proved

Z/28—See How They Ran

Year	Carburetion	0–60 (sec)	Quarter Mile	Top Speed	Magazine
1967	1x4 Holley	6.7	14.9/97	124 mph	C&D 5/67
1967	1x4 Holley	6.9	14.9/100	132 mph	R&T 6/68
1968	1x4 Holley	7.4	14.85/101.4	133 mph	CL 7/68
1968	2x4 Holley	5.3	13.77/107.39	132 mph	C&D 7/68
1969	1x4 Holley	7.1	15.0/96	—	SCG 6/69
1969	2x4 Holley	7.4	15.12/94.8	133 mph	CL 8/69
1969	2x4 Holley	—	12.8/116 *	—	SCG 5/70

Penske Trans-Am racer

C&D = Car and Driver   R&T = Road & Track   CL = Car Life   SCG = Sports Car Graphic

The Z/28 could be a stormer at the drags if the driver knew how to keep the rpms up and launch the car properly. *Car Life* magazine clicked off a 15.12/94.8 mph in stock form with Cross Ram dual quads. Minor modifications like headers and slicks could pull ETs down into the 13s.

The Donohue Legend

Although Mark Donohue had already established himself as an up and coming driver, it was his incredible performance in the 1967–1969 SCCA Trans-Am series that cemented his legacy. Donohue was on the grid for 55 Trans-Am races, capturing 23 poles. He won 29 races and placed in the top three 43 times. In 1968 alone he scored a record 10 wins out of 13 events and brought Chevrolet the first of its two Manufacturer's titles (1968–1969).

itself to be a spectacular power plant. On the street, the 302 was cantankerous in cold weather and was undriveable below 3000 rpms. The driver had to constantly keep rowing the Hurst shifter back and forth through the gears to keep the rpms up.

For 1969, the Special Performance Package was basically unchanged from 1968; however, the 302 engine received a few internal improvements. The block now had thicker main bearing webs, four-bolt mains, and a large journal crankshaft. The intake manifold was redesigned and the water pump assembly was longer and deeper. While headers (Z/282) and plenum air induction (Z/284) options had been cancelled during 1968, they were still offered over the counter for 1969.

Externally, there was no question when one was driving a Z/28. If the wide "Stereo Stripes" didn't register, there were large "Z/28" emblems adorning the front fenders. Early production Z/28s had the 1968-style decklid stripes and spoilers. The 1968 production spoilers were slightly shorter than the wider 1969 rear and weren't replaced by second-production units until October 1968. Inside, when a tachometer was ordered, it had a 7000-rpm limit and a 6000-rpm redline. These were replaced with 8000-rpm tachometers with 6500-rpm redlines during the model year. The D80 rear decklid spoiler and front chin spoiler were now included in the Z/28 package. For those who wanted to drive the boulevard more incognito, the wide stripes could be deleted.

In mid-December, Chevrolet released the RPO ZL2 Special Ducted Hood (known as the "Super Scoop") as a $79 option. The ZL2 hood, designed by Larry Shinoda, featured a high-rise section in the center that ended with a rearward-facing duct that drew high-pressure air from the cowl into the carburetor through an underhood plenum. The factory ZL2 hoods were stamped steel with special bracings around the round plenum opening that allowed the air cleaner to fit within. The

Heavy-Duty Service fiberglass hood was available over the counter for use with the cross ram. It used the same cowl induction technique as the production hood; however, the underhood was molded specifically to mate to the foam seal that surrounded the dual carbs. An adapter package was released to use the Heavy-Duty Service hood with the four-barrel setup.

Aside from the Corvette, the Camaro and the Z/28 were the only American production cars in 1969 to offer four-wheel disc brakes. The Camaro setup (RPO JL8) cost around $500 and was plagued with OE supplier parts problems. That shortage made delivery difficult and kept bumping the price of the option upwards. Consequently, only 206 sets of four-wheel discs were installed at the factory when the option was canceled in mid-July1969. A Heavy-Duty Service four-wheel brake package was also offered over the counter. Savvy option manipulators who wanted the strongest setup for racing could order the RPO JL8 brake package on the car and the Heavy-Duty Service four-wheel brake package over the counter and install the Heavy-Duty Service rear axle assembly in place of the JL8's rear axle. The benefit was to utilize the larger diameter axle shafts and bearings, which were better suited for the rigors of racing.

Pilot 1969 Z/28 gleams under the lights in the GM Styling Studio auditorium. Pre-production car wears correct badges and emblems.

For 1969, Z/28 badges appeared on front fenders.

Z/28 badge appeared on tail lamp panel. Fuel filler was moved to location behind the license plate.

Blacked out grille featured Z/28 badge next to LH headlamp.

Z/28 engine compartment with standard log-style exhaust manifolds and seven-fin cast aluminum valve covers.

Z/28 engine compartment. Note factory headers and air cleaner with snorkel and foam sealer to mate with cold air hood. Wire to underhood is lead to solenoid that operates door in cold air hood.

Racing

With one Trans-Am championship under their belts, Penske Racing was considered a strong contender to repeat their amazing 1968 season. The team had built two new 1969 Z/28 Camaros for the season. However, testing at Chevrolet's Research & Development center revealed considerable teething problems with the new cars.

Mark Donohue not only was sorting out the problems with the cars, but he had also taken on the duties of team manager, handling

much of the logistics of running the team's operations as well as driving. The team was in the third and last year of its contract with Chevrolet, and the rift between Piggins and Penske had worsened. Penske's attention had turned to other projects and challenges, and some of them displeased Chevrolet, who felt Penske should continue to be involved personally in the team's day-to-day activities.

The Penske team struggled through the first five races, losing for reasons ranging from errors in race strategy to mechanical failures. The cooperation level between engineers at Chevrolet Research & Development and the Penske team was fortunately still intact, and much of the telemetry Chevrolet Engineer Don Gates gathered from the race cars was translated into information Donohue and his second driver, Ronnie Bucknum, could utilize to improve lap times. Don Cox had built a "racing mule" that allowed him to simulate much of the dynamics of stress the Camaros underwent during racing, and his input was invaluable to Donohue. It was Cox who discovered that switching the master cylinder brake lines to utilize the opposite cylinder reservoirs solved the braking problems that had plagued the car. The application of this data resulted in immediate success.

RPO D80 was still a $32 option on the Z/28, added front valance and rear deck spoilers.

Phases and Changes

The Z/28 option package went through a variety of configurations during the extended 1969 model year, which lasted from the car's introduction in September 1968 to the end of the model run in February 1970. Changes were made primarily to the exhaust and brake systems:

Z/28 Option Package
Dated September 26, 1968

Includes 302-inch V8 engine, dual exhaust with deep tone mufflers, special front and rear suspension, rear bumper guards, heavy-duty radiator and temperature-controlled fan, quick ratio steering, 15 x 7 rally wheels, E70 x 15 special white-lettered tires, 3.73:1 ratio axle, and special rally stripes on hood and rear deck. Available only when four-speed transmission and power disc brakes are ordered. Positraction rear axle recommended. Package price $458.15

Z/28 Option Package
Dated October 18, 1968

Includes 302-inch V8 engine with bright accents; chambered dual exhaust system; Z/28 emblems on grille, front fender and rear panel; special front and rear suspension; rear bumper guards; heavy-duty radiator and temperature-controlled fan; quick ratio steering; 15 x 7 wheels with trim rings; E70 x 15 special white-lettered blackwall tires; and special paint stripes on hood and rear deck. Available only when four-speed transmission and power front or four-wheel disc brakes are ordered. Positraction rear axle recommended. JL-8 (four-wheel discs) recommended. Package price $458.15

Z/28 Option Package
Dated January 2, 1969

Includes 302-inch V8 engine with bright accents; dual exhaust; Z/28 emblems on grille, front fender, and rear panel; special front and rear suspension; rear bumper guards; heavy-duty radiator and temperature-controlled fan; quick ratio steering; stripes on 15 x 7 wheels with trim rings; E70 x 15 special white-lettered blackball tires; and special paint hood and rear deck. Available only when tachometer gauge or special instrumentation, four-speed transmission and power front or four-wheel disc brakes are ordered. Positraction rear axle recommended. JL-8 (four-wheel discs) recommended. Package price $473.95

Z/28 Option Package
Dated April 1, 1969

Includes 302-inch V8 engine with bright accents; chambered dual exhaust system; Z/28 emblems on grille, front fender, and rear panel; special front and rear suspension; rear bumper guards; heavy-duty radiator and temperature-controlled fan; quick ratio steering; 15 x 7 wheels with special center caps and trim rings; E70 x 15 special white-lettered blackwall tires; auxiliary front valance panel and rear deck spoiler; and special paint stripes on hood and rear deck. Available only when four-speed transmission and power front or four-wheel disc brakes are ordered. Positraction rear axle recommended. Package price $506.15

Z/28 Option Package
Dated September 18, 1969

Includes 302-inch V8 engine with bright accents; dual exhausts with bright tips; Z/28 emblems on grille, front fender, and rear panel; special front and rear suspension; rear bumper guards; heavy-duty radiator and temperature-controlled fan; quick ratio steering; 15 x 7 wheels with special center caps and trim rings; E70 x 15 special white-lettered blackwall tires; auxiliary front valance panel and rear deck spoiler; and special paint stripes on hood and rear deck. Available only when tachometer gauge or special instrumentation, four-speed transmission and power front disc brakes are ordered. Positraction rear axle recommended. Package price $522.40

Z/28 Option Package
Dated November 3, 1969

Includes 302-inch V8 engine with bright accents; dual exhausts with bright tips; Z/28 emblems on grille, front fender, and rear panel; special front and rear suspension; rear bumper guards; heavy-duty radiator and temperature-controlled fan; quick ratio steering; 15 x 7 wheels with special center caps and trim rings; E70 x 15 special white-lettered blackwall tires; auxiliary front valance panel and rear deck spoiler; and special paint stripes on hood and rear deck. Available only when tachometer gauge or special instrumentation, four-speed transmission and power front disc brakes are ordered. Positraction rear axle recommended. Package price $522.40

Top: Wide and dramatic look of 1969 Z/28 is emphasized by bold twin stripes and V-shaped grille.

Ford had invested big money in the Boss 302 racing teams and had funded five cars between two teams headed by Carroll Shelby and Bud Moore. The Mustang teams were constantly testing and, just by the sheer presence of Ford money, were highly competitive. Chevrolet, on the other hand, could not finance—even covertly—any racing operations. They could provide research and homologate componentry to improve the breed, but not a dollar went into paying the expenses of fielding a race car. Fortunately, Penske had other sponsors, especially Sun Oil, but even the aggregate dollars from these other sponsors didn't add up to the money Ford was spending.

This disparity in sponsorship, combined with the bad luck that plagued the Penske team in the first half of the season, only added to their frustration. There was also an ugly atmosphere within the Trans-Am that season. The Ford teams were constantly complaining about Penske's ability to read the SCCA rule book and find "unfair advantages" to give them a leg up on the competition. Not only was the Ford contingent upset, SCCA officials didn't care for Donohue and Company sliding these advantages under the judges and stewards' noses and expecting to be approved. To some SCCA Trans-Am officials, Penske's team was arrogant and cocksure, and they weren't going to let the racers have the last word. A good example was the vinyl roofs that adorned the Penske cars.

Cross ram installed in 1968 Z/28 with over the counter fiberglass Heavy Duty Service ZL2 hood. Note hood pin posts in top of core support. Engineering used the bracket bolted to the RH hood hinge for some unknown purpose.

1969 Z/28. The Z/28 enjoyed its best sales volume in 1969, selling 20,302 copies.

Boss 302 vs. Z/28

The Chevy/Ford war that Piggins had envisioned had come to pass, and by 1969 the Z/28 had fulfilled its mission as a Mustang beater on and off the track. Ford had underestimated the Z/28's potential and was stymied by Chevrolet's success with its small-block screamer. Ironically, it took two former GM executives to develop a worthy competitor to the Z/28.

Semon "Bunkie" Knudsen had spent his career at GM, saving Pontiac in the fifties, running Chevrolet in the early sixties and then ascending to corporate vice president. In line for the GM presidency in the late sixties, Knudsen was disconcerted when he was passed over in favor of Ed Cole. In February 1968, Knudsen jumped when Henry Ford II offered him the top spot at Ford with the assignment to change Ford's image with young musclecar buyers. Knudsen brought with him to Ford the talents of designer Larry Shinoda, who had to his styling credit such jewels as the 1963 Corvette and the Z/28.

Ford's strong commitment to racing in the sixties had earned them stock car championships and victories at Indianapolis, LeMans, and the new Trans-Am series. What Ford couldn't do was translate those victories into sales of high-performance cars. The Z/28 was an excellent example of GM's ability to do just that. To take advantage of the heated competition of the Trans-Am series, Knudsen knew Ford's solution was to counter what Chevrolet had done with the Z/28 and do it better. For Ford, their 1968 302 Tunnel Port Trans-Am engine had been a disaster. The huge round port heads required more volumetric airflow than the engine's displacement could supply, limiting the power band to the higher rpm ranges. The first order of business was to develop a new engine and build a special Mustang around it to image on the street and race on the tracks.

Ford Engineering had been working on a new 351-cubic inch engine for 1970 release that used canted valve heads similar to Chevrolet's "Porcupine" heads. The canted placement of the big valves (2.23-inch intake and 1.71-inch exhaust) allowed for straighter passages and better airflow. These "Cleveland" heads (so named for the Cleveland foundry where they were produced) were grafted to the thickly webbed 302 block. A high-rise aluminum intake manifold topped by a 780-cfm Holley was added to produce results far superior to the Tunnel Port. Ford had developed a worthy competitor to Chevrolet's 302 engine.

Shinoda's job was to transform the Mach 1 Mustang into a lean and mean racer. He was also instrumental in naming this new Trans-Am Mustang "Boss 302." His brilliant modifications of the Mach 1 included removing the side scoops and horse medallions, designing aggressive side stripes, and adding dramatic matte black highlights to the front, hood, and rear. Shinoda also added a 45-degree chin spoiler, a rear deck wing, and black slatted "Sports Roof" over the backlight.

Using the Z/28 as the target allowed Ford to built a superb performance car. The Boss 302 exceeded the Z/28 in many regards, especially in suspension, brakes, and tire application. The Boss 302 engine was beefier than the Z/28 and more driveable on the street. With Knudsen's intuitive feeling for the marketplace and an appreciation for racing (he had put Pontiac on top of NASCAR in the early sixties), the Boss 302 was a brawny boulevard fighter that had the suds to go *mano a mano* with the Z/28. After driving the Boss 302, *Car and Driver* said, "Ford's answer to the Z/28 rates an A."

Although the Boss came to market late—it was April 17, 1969, when the first Boss 302s were assembled—the hype in the showroom between the Boss 302 and the Z/28 was as aggressive as the door-banging, fender-bashing action on the Trans-Am track. Ford hit the 1,000 unit sold mark on May 11 and ended 1969 production with 1,628 units sold. Although the Boss 302 hardly put a dent in the Z/28's 1969 sales of 20,302 units, it did prove that Ford had learned how to sell what they raced. Ironically, it wasn't long after the Boss's release that Henry Ford II fired Knudsen, but not before the Boss 302 left its mark.

Boss 302's graphics were bold and plentiful, with standup rear deck wing, front chin spoiler, and shaded "sports roof." Tom Shaw photo

Tale of the Tape—Boss 302 vs. Z/28

Dimensions	Z/28	Boss 302
Wheelbase (inches)	108.1	108.0
Width (inches)	74.0	71.8
Height (inches)	51.6	50.4
Overall length (inches)	186.0	187.4
Tread (inches)		
Front	59.6	57.5
Rear	59.5	57.5
Curb weight (lbs.)	3455	3250

Engine		
Type	V8	V8
Displacement	302	302
Bore & stroke	4.00 x 3.00	4.00 x 3.00
Horsepower	290 @ 5800	290 @ 5800
Torque	290 @ 4200	290 @ 4300
Compression ratio	11.0:1	10.5:1
Block	cast iron	cast iron
Heads	cast iron	cast iron

Z/28 wore wide stripes, front and rear spoilers, and cold air hood.

Engine *(continued)*

Valve diameter (int./ex.) (inches)	2.02/1.60	2.23/1.71
Intake manifold	cast aluminum	cast aluminum
Crankshaft	forged steel	forged steel
Rods	forged steel	forged steel
Pistons	aluminum	aluminum
Carburetion	800 cfm Holley	780 cfm Holley

Drivetrain

Transmission	Muncie M21	Ford Top Loader
Rear axle ratio	3.73:1	3.50:1

Chassis

Suspension

Front suspension	SLA, coil spring	SLA, coil spring
Shock absorber	direct acting	direct acting
Shock absorber piston diameter (inches)	1.00	1.1875
Front spring rate (lb. per inch)	320	350
Front stabilizer bar diameter (inch)	.685	.85
Rear suspension	multileaf spring	multileaf spring

Engine compartment of Boss 302. Chrome air cleaner and valve covers were part of the Boss 302 package. Rev limiter was used to prevent grenading the block at super-high rpms.

Suspension (continued)		
Rear spring size (inches)	56. x 2.50	53. x 2.50
Rear spring rate (lb. per inch)	125	150
Shock absorber placement	staggered	staggered
Steering		
Type	recirculating ball	recirculating ball
Ratio	17.5:1	16:1
Turns lock-to-lock	2.8	3.74
Turning circle (dia. ft.)	37.0	37.6
Brakes		
Standard	front disc/rear drum	front disc/rear drum
Swept area (sq. inches)	332.4	282.5
Front disc diameter (inches)	11.0	11.3
Rear drum diameter (inches)	9.5	10.0
Wheels	stamped steel 15 x 7	stamped steel 15 x 7
Tires	E70 x 15	F60 x 15
Performance		
Quarter-Mile	14.34/101.35 mph *	14.57/97.57 mph +
	Hot Rod 1/69	*+ Car and Driver 6/69*

Both the Z/28 and the Boss 302 engines were rated at 290 horsepower@5800 rpm.

The controversy that developed over the vinyl roofs used on the Penske cars provides a good example of the animosity between Penske's and Ford's teams and the SCCA. Before the cars had been built, the bodies had been acid dipped. This was no secret; all the teams did it for weight saving. Unfortunately, the Penske cars stayed "in the tank" a little too long and the tops were wrinkled. Penske concluded it would be cheaper to hide the wrinkles by covering the roofs with correct factory vinyl tops, right down to the bright trim moldings rather than hacking off the roofs and welding on new ones. It was also more economical to cover the roofs than having to paint them along with the rest of the car before each race. The other teams screamed foul and forced SCCA to ban vinyl tops in midseason. Penske protested and held his cars out until a last-minute compromise was reached. In the end, Penske Racing welded new roofs on the cars.

The harassment from the SCCA, ranging from Penske's pit gas tank to the vinyl tops, was one thing. The charges of cheating, made right to Penske's face by Ford drivers, was another. These accusations were enough to galvanize Penske's determination that his team would now

Penske Racing repeated its winning ways in 1969, winning the Manufacturer's Championship again. It would be the last year for Penske's Trans-Am relationship with Chevrolet.

One of the most famous Z/28 magazine covers was this *Car Life* issue from August 1969. Editor Allan Girdler drives a Daytona Yellow Z/28 with Yellow Houndstooth Custom interior. Note absence of 302 badge on Super Scoop.

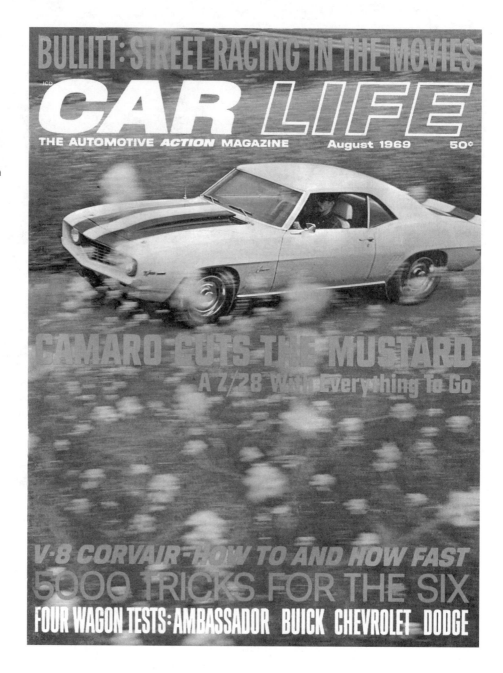

BULLITT: STREET RACING IN THE MOVIES

CAR LIFE

THE AUTOMOTIVE *ACTION* MAGAZINE   August 1969   50¢

CAMARO CUTS THE MUSTARD
A Z/28 With Everything To Go

V-8 CORVAIR-HOW TO AND HOW FAST
5000 TRICKS FOR THE SIX
FOUR WAGON TESTS: AMBASSADOR BUICK CHEVROLET DODGE

Z is for "Zap!"

Translation: a 302 V8 with mechanical lifters, hi-performance cam, aluminum intake manifold, Holley 4-barrel.

Plus: multi-leaf rear springs, heavy-duty shocks, new white-lettered tires on 15 x 7 wheels.

And a Hurst shifter for the 4-speed.

While you're at it, why not add the new 'Vette type 4-wheel disc brakes?

By now you know the mean streak isn't just painted on—it's built in.

CHEVROLET

Putting you first, keeps us first.

We've got a mean streak.

Z/28 Camaro.

1969 Camaro "Mean Streak" ad was brash and to the point in announcing the Z/28's performance parts.

spend whatever time and money it took to win the 1969 Trans-Am series. Actually, this "circle the wagons" policy wasn't so much done to win the season as it was to thoroughly beat the Mustang contingent and the SCCA at the same time. For the cool and reserved Penske, it was no longer business—it was personal. For Penske Racing, the business at hand now was to win.

The Mustang teams fought hard on the track, with Parnelli Jones winning four out of the first five races. Then, incredibly, the two Mustang teams made it easy for Penske by self-destructing, wiping out four of the five cars in one accident at St. Jovite, the seventh race of the series. For the first time, the Camaro led the points series, 49 to Mustang's 46.

Between Donohue and Bucknum, the Penske team had won five straight races by the tenth event at Kent. Two weeks later at Sears Point, Chevrolet clinched the championship as Donohue beat Jones again. At the final race, it was a melee as all five Mustang team cars ground against the two Penske Camaros. Jones and Donohue battled bumper-to-bumper and wheel-to-wheel, ending in both cars spinning off the track. Donohue was able to recover and win the race, but Jones' car was done for the day. At the end, three of the Mustangs were DF, the remaining two finishing fourth and ninth. The final points standing was Camaro 78, Mustang 64.

Although Penske and Donohue had beaten Ford and won the championship, the costs had been high. The following year Penske Racing would be sponsored by American Motors. The intense rivalry between manufacturers and teams would never be as pitched as it was in 1969. The Penske victories were tributes to Chevrolet Engineering's hard work in designing the Z/28 engines and componentry and its use of state of the art computer technology to assist the driver/engineer in dialing in the race cars. It was also the perseverance and dedication to detail that was the mark of the Penske organization. To win without factory money was indicative of Penske's obsession with the business of winning. It's unfortunate that the Chevrolet/Penske combination couldn't have continued in Trans-Am racing.

Although difficult, the 1967–1969 series paid off for Mark Donohue, Roger Penske, and Chevrolet. To add to his incredible talents as a driver, Donohue learned race car technology and how to translate that knowledge into building and driving winning cars. For the Penske organization, the lessons learned from the Trans-Am series would be the foundation for winning teams in a number of racing venues, including the Indianapolis 500, for the next three decades.

For Chevrolet, the Trans-Am series had been the mission accomplished. Vince Piggins' job had been to put the Camaro on the map and prove it was more than GM's "me too" ponycar. He, with the enormous support of Chevrolet, had demonstrated that the Camaro, in its street and race configurations, was more then the Mustang's equal. It was truly a legend in its time.

All aluminum ZL1 427 was the heart of the COPO 9560 package. At 430 horse-power, the ZL1 was virtually identical to the L88 except for the camshaft profile.

Chapter Six

Variations on a Theme—The Ultimate Camaros

When the 1967 Camaro was released to the public, the first thing drag racers did was take a tape measure to the engine compartment to see if a big block would fit. They were delighted to discover the Camaro was the first lightweight Chevrolet product that would accept a big block without massive front-end modification. Two months later, Chevrolet released the L35 325-horsepower 396 engine for the Camaro. Most factory brochures and sales albums specified the L35 as the only available big-block option. Knowledgeable buyers or plugged-in dealers knew of other 396 RPO numbers that delivered up to 375 horsepower. These engines could be factory-installed with the full General Motors powertrain warranty. Because of GM's horsepower-to-weight ratio limits (roughly 11 pounds curb weight per horsepower), the 375-horsepower was pushing the corporate envelope as far as permissible.

That GM policy did not apply to dealers, however. The late sixties was the era of high performance, and enthusiasts wanted more muscle in their musclecars. Several dozen Chevrolet dealers catered to their customer's desire to peel the paint off every comer at the stoplight Grand Prix. These dealers had found high performance to be a profitable part of their business. Dealers like Megrollis Chevrolet in Detroit, Roger Penske Chevrolet in Philadelphia, Jack Head Chevrolet in Los Angeles, and Ammon Smith Chevrolet in York, Pennsylvania, all took the same approach—installing more cubes. Dealers and drag racers were anxious to order a Camaro with the 427 in place of the 396, but they had to settle for dealer or customer installations in 1967 and 1968.

Even though Chevrolet was obligated to follow the corporate standards for horsepower-to-weight on all of its vehicles, the rules were bent to accommodate a few dealers that wanted either to go drag racing or to sell to individual racers. Drag racers were itching to take a 427-equipped Camaro into NHRA's stock classes and just clean house. To satisfy this demand, in 1969 Chevrolet built two special runs of Camaros equipped with the 427 engine. These were the Ultimate Camaros.

COPO

It's vital that the 427 Camaro story begins at Chevrolet's Central Office. The 1967 Camaro hadn't been on the street long before demand for a 427-powered Camaro began filtering in from a handful of Chevrolet dealers who specialized in high performance. Chevrolet Product Promotions Manager Vince Piggins was anxious to get 427 Camaros into the hands of drag racers but was stymied by GM's horsepower-to-weight edict for production cars.

Chevrolet did have the ability to produce special vehicles in limited quantities for customers by using a Central Office Production Order (COPO). A COPO could be used to build an armada of Chevrolet taxis optioned out in a specific manner for a corporate customer or a fleet of yellow buses for a school district. It could also be used to circumvent the horsepower-to-weight edict by building a run of COPO 427 Camaros for a dealer.

There is evidence that Yenko Chevrolet had the inside track on ordering 427 Camaros from the factory in 1968, thanks to a covert COPO that Piggins personally approved. For appearance's sake and to prevent other dealers from crying foul, Don Yenko still claimed to have done all of his 427 installations himself.

The secret 1968 program proved to be successful, and, combined with more dealers clamoring for factory-built 427 Camaros, three "High-Performance Unit" COPOs were written for the 1969 Camaro. For drag racers, an all-aluminum 427, designated ZL1, was built. Rated at 430 horsepower @ 5200 rpm and 450 lb-ft torque @ 4400 rpm, the ZL1 required super high octane to satisfy its 12.0:1 high compression craving.

For street performance as well as drag racing, COPO 9561 delivered the L72 iron version of the 427 that cranked 425 horsepower @ 5600 rpm and 460 lb-ft at 4000 rpm. The third order was COPO 9737, the "Special Sport Car Conversion/Yenko" package, which consisted of a hefty one-inch front anti-roll bar, E70 x 15 tires on 15 x 7-inch ZJ7 Rally Wheels, special UPC 12 fuel gauge and a 140 mph speedometer. Any dealer could order COPO 9737 with either the ZL1 or the L72.

What Did a COPO Consist Of?

The COPO 9560 package consisted of an all aluminum ZL1 427 engine, ZL2 cold air hood, four-core radiator, transistorized ignition, cast iron, heavy service 12-bolt differential, multi-leaf rear springs, and 4.10:1 Positraction rear axle with heat-treated ring and pinion. In appearance, the engine block, heads, and intake were left natural aluminum. All other engine parts were painted black.

The COPO 9561 package consisted of the L72 iron block and heads 427 engine, aluminum intake and bellhousing, four-core radiator, ZL2 cold air hood, heavy service 12-bolt differential, multileaf rear springs, and 4.10:1 Positraction rear axle with heat-treated ring and pinion. The engine was painted Chevrolet Engine Orange.

Mandatory options for both packages were power front disc brakes and either the Muncie four-speed manual gearbox or the M40 three-speed Turbo Hydra-Matic. Both packages were adorned with the base Camaro emblems. On Yenko models, the bow tie emblem in the grille center was removed and replaced with Yenko badges.

Dover White 1969 COPO 9560 Camaro. A total of 69 were ordered, most of them placed by Fred Gibb Chevrolet. Note absence of bright trim moldings and only the "Camaro" nameplate on the front fender. Blue bow tie emblem is in center of Argent Silver grille.

COPO 9561 delivered the 425-horsepower L72 427 engine. The L72 was made with an iron block and heads. Intake manifold is cast aluminum.

COPO Production

COPO Order Number	Transmission	Quantity
9560 AA	Four-speed	47*
9560 BA	Automatic	22
9561 AA	Four-Speed	822
9561 BA	Automatic	193

* 34 M21 and 13 M22.

Two dealers were at the forefront of the COPO 9560 and 9561 programs. Yenko Chevrolet purchased more 9561 Camaros than any other dealer. Fred Gibb Chevrolet was instrumental in creation of the COPO 9560 ZL1 Camaros for drag racing.

Don Yenko

Don Yenko was a true enthusiast. He loved to race Corvettes and he loved to build high-performance Chevrolets for his customers. Located in Cannonsburg, Pennsylvania, Yenko Chevrolet became the Mecca for those seeking 427 Corvettes, Camaros, and Chevelles.

Special "SYC" logo appeared on the headrests of 1969 Yenko Camaros.

Yenko had a distribution system that sold SYC Camaros all over the country. How many SYC Camaros were sold via other dealers is not documented.

1967 Yenko Camaro in Tuxedo Black. Note special fiberglass hood that features Corvette-style hood with cowl induction and hood pins.

Special emblems for the 1967 Yenko included dealer badge and 427 nameplate.

In 1967, Yenko would pull the 396 out of your new Yenko Camaro and install a 427. He not only installed the 425-horsepower 427 big block, he also added some other pieces to the package, like a lightweight hood with functional scoop, tachometer strapped to the steering column, extra gauges, and Pontiac Rally II wheels with the "Y" Yenko emblem in the center cap. Yenko exterior badges rounded out the package. Yenko understood how important it was that his Super Camaros not only ran like the devil but also looked good. Records indicate that Yenko made 54 Camaro conversions in 1967.

Yenko used the Pontiac rally II wheel as part of the Yenko package in 1967. He replaced the PMD nameplate in the center cap with custom "Y" emblems.

1968 Yenko with SS package, Z21 Style Trim Group and CO82 Black Vinyl Top. Yenko-designed fiberglass hood featured new, "ram air" style hood scoops.

1968 Yenko Camaro. Note 427 and Yenko emblems on either side of the fuel filler.

L72 427 iron big block boasted 425 horsepower in stock form. Taller, open air cleaner assembly matched Yenko's custom hood.

For 1968, the Yenko Camaro didn't require a conversion; the factory built his cars as a COPO. Besides saving him the conversion time, the cars were also emissions correct. There was little change to the Yenko Camaro for 1968. It still featured the same hood, emblems, and wheels as in 1967, although he began offering more accessories. Yenko sold 68

427 1968 Camaros either at his dealership or to other dealers through Span, his distribution system based in the Midwest.

The big change came in January 1969 with the introduction of the Super Yenko Camaro (SYC). Yenko could not process orders from customers and other dealers fast enough, so he negotiated with Chevrolet for a run of 100 L72 427 Camaros. These were the COPO 9561 Camaros. Yenko took delivery of the cars and added special exterior stripes (the customer could request the stripes be deleted), Yenko nameplates, SYC emblems on the headrests, and a Stewart Warner tachometer strapped to the steering column (later replaced by a factory in-dash tachometer). The SYC Camaro was base priced at $4245. From there, the buyer had a choice of either the M40 Turbo Hydra-Matic or Muncie M22 Rockcrusher four-speed transmission as well as a brace of other options.

Yenko went through the first 100 cars and placed a second order for 101 additional COPO 9561 Camaros in November 1969. He calculated this would be enough to carry him through since the 1969 model run would be extended to February 1970.

Early 1969 Camaro with Yenko package shows 1968-style ducktail spoiler, which was approximately two inches short on each side. Yenko and 427 nameplates appear in the blacked-out tail lamp.

Dick Harrell at the wheel of the Yenko Super Camaro, nose to nose with Tasca Ford's "Mystery 8" Mustang. Harrell built funny cars for several dealers.

Fred Gibb

Tucked away in LaHarpe, Illinois, Fred Gibb had a small Chevrolet store and a burning passion to drag race. Gibb started racing in 1967 with a Z/28 and retired at the top in 1971, taking the AHRA Pro Stock World championship. Many pay tribute to Gibb as the "father of the ZL1" since he worked with Vince Piggins to develop the package and then stood up to the plate and ordered 50 COPO 9560 ZL1 427 Camaros for his dealership.

That huge order turned out to be a terrible mistake. Gibb's enthusiasm for the package overshadowed his business sense, and he was not prepared for the whopping $7,200 sticker on each car. When the floor plan bill arrived, Gibb had not been able to move all of the ZL1s he had in stock because of their pricey sticker. Gibb was able to get Chevrolet's Central Office to disburse 37 of the 50 cars he had to other dealers. Chevrolet

The Inner Workings

Just what made up a ZL1? Built at the Tonawanda engine plant (home of the Chevrolet big block), the ZL1 started with a T356 aluminum alloy block with iron cylinder liners. The big-valve aluminum heads featured open chambers and rectangular-shaped ports. For the high rpms the ZL1 would turn, engineers specified a Tuftrided steel crank and solid lifter cam (.560-inch intake/.600-inch exhaust) and special forged rods with 12:1 forged aluminum pistons. The ZL1 inhaled through a Holley 850 double pumper on a high-rise, dual-plane aluminum intake manifold and exhaled through cast iron 396 exhaust manifolds.

received an additional 19 COPO 9560 orders from various other dealers, resulting in a total of 69 COPO 9560 Camaros built in 1969.

Dick Harrell took the first COPO 9560 delivered to Gibb back to his Kansas City shop in early January 1969 and modified it for AHRA S/S racing. The ZL1's debut at the 1969 AHRA Winternationals at Phoenix was spectacular. Driven by Herb Fox (a Gibb Chevrolet mechanic), the ZL1 made it to the semifinals by beating Ronnie Sox's Hemi 'Cuda. Arlen Venke in a 1969 Hemi 'Cuda beat Fox in the finals and went on to take the Super Stock Eliminator trophy. In all, it was a pretty auspicious entry into drag racing competition.

Numerous dealers participated in the COPO 9560 and 9561 programs; however, most of them ordered one or two cars at most. Many were content to sell the customer a new big-block Camaro, jerk the 396 (and later sell it for more profit), and charge the customer for the 427 installation.

The other benefit to having a dealer install a 427 was that it allowed the customer to design the engine for his application and budget. Dual quads and even three deuces were offered, along with special suspension and other options.

Of all these performance dealers, four stand out: Berger Chevrolet, Nickey Chevrolet, Baldwin-Motion, and Dana Chevrolet.

Berger

Berger Chevrolet had long been one of those "with it" dealers that sold high performance Chevrolets. It had also become a source for high-performance parts in the Grand Rapids area of Michigan. With the addition of local drag racing star Jim Luikens, Berger stepped up its advertising in national magazines and began writing performance parts orders from all over the country. Along with building some 427 Camaros for customers, Berger sold one 9650 and also ordered 50 9561 COPO Camaros for sale through the dealership.

Nickey

Located in the Chicago suburbs, Nickey Chevrolet had developed a strong over-the-counter high-performance parts program and sponsored several racing team efforts. The dealership commissioned California's master engine builder Bill Thomas to assemble a 427 Camaro package for street and strip. The AHRA recognized these 427 Camaros for Super Stock competition, while the NHRA did not. The installation of the engine or the purchase of a 427 Camaro could be arranged either in Chicago at the Nickey dealership or at Thomas' facility in Southern California.

The package started with the customer purchasing a Nickey SS350 Camaro with metallic brakes, M21 four speed, and Positraction differential and then turning it over to the service department for the installation of the 427. Traction bars and polished Cragar SS wheels were also part of the package, which totaled out at a very reasonable $3,711.65. Those who wanted more could chose individual components or Nickey performance kits that ranged from $389 to $1,089 and included dual quads or the Corvette's three deuces.

It wasn't unusual for Nickey to leave the SS350 badge in the grille and bolt a small 427 emblem to the front fender behind the wheel opening. A Nickey badge was affixed to the tail lamp panel. In 1968, the Nickey nameplate replaced the SS badge on the front fenders (inside the stripe), making it a real sleeper.

By 1969, Nickey offered several 427 Camaro packages, starting with the L72, the L88 and even a Z/28 with a L72 replacing the 302.

Blasts from the Past—427 Style

Year	Model	Carburetion	Quarter-Mile	Magazine
1967	Dana	1 x 4 Holley	14.2/102 mph	CL 4/67
1967	Nickey	2 x 4 AFB	13.9/108 mph	C&D 9/67
1968	Nickey	2 x 4 Holley	11.43/124 mph	PHR 6/68
1968	Motion	1 x 4 Holley	11.5/125 mph	HPC 3/68
1969	ZL1	1 x 4 Holley	11.78/122.50 mph	PHR 7/69

CL = Car Life   C&D = Car and Driver   PHR = Popular Hot Rodding   HPC = High Performance Cars

While Nickey Chevrolet in Chicago got little editorial coverage, they ran full-page ads in enthusiast press for their 427 Camaro conversions and performance parts business.

Baldwin Motion

Located on Long Island, New York, Baldwin Chevrolet teamed with Motion Performance to represent the "bad boys" of performance dealers. Their unabashed devotion to street racing produced 500-horsepower screamers that not only would decimate any Hemi on the Bronx Cross-town Expressway but that also came with a warranty!

Here's how the Baldwin-Motion partnership worked: A customer bought his Chevrolet product at Baldwin Chevrolet (financed just like at any other Chevy store) and took it to Motion Performance for modification. Under the direction of Joel Rosen, Motion Performance built astonishingly powerful street cars that could be driven to the dragstrip and then proceed to blow away everything in their class. Rosen had developed a series of packages for the Camaro that culminated in the "Phase 3." Depending on what the customer wanted, Rosen could deliver up to 500 horsepower using his favorite engine, the 425-horsepower, 427 and

Baldwin/Motion combined to sell and build some of the wildest street Camaros available anywhere. Depending on customer choice, Motion could build up to 600-horsepower street engines in 1967.

THE QUICKEST AND FASTEST SUPERCAR! SS-427 CAMARO

DYNO-TUNED AND READY TO WAIL...$3,650.00

STANDARD EQUIPMENT:
★ 425-HP 427 ENGINE ★ CLOSE-RATIO MUNCIE FOUR-SPEED ★ POSITRACTION REAR ★ HD SUSPENSION ★ HD RADIATOR ★ TRACTION BARS ★ REDLINE WIDE OVAL TIRES ★ CHROME VALVE COVERS ★ DISTINCTIVE EMBLEMS ★ STRIPING ★ MODIFIED IGNITION ★ BUCKET SEATS
FULLY COVERED BY WARRANTY!
AVAILABLE ON SPECIAL ORDER! ALL FACTORY HIGH-PERFORMANCE OPTIONS
★ TRI-POWER ★ DISC BRAKES ★ HEADERS ★ MAG WHEELS ★ DEEP PAN ★ STREET ENGINES TO 600 HP

BOLT-ON SUPER-BITE SUSPENSION KITS!

Designed and engineered by Motion Performance for its SS-427 Camaro, this street-strip kit is the last word in supercar ride and traction control. Each kit contains four CUSTOM-VALVED Cure Ride shocks, front coil spring risers and SUPER-DUTY bolt-on 1/4-inch steel bar stock traction bars. These bars are standard equipment on the SS-427 Motion Camaro and are guaranteed to stop axle and spring windup and wheel hop regardless of tires and engine output. Available ONLY from Motion Performance, Inc.

BOLT-ON KIT FOR CAMAROS AND FIREBIRDS...RACER'S NET $ 99.88
TRACTION BARS ONLY ....RACER'S NET $ 49.95
BOLT-ON KITS FOR MUSTANGS AND HP FORDS.RACER'S NET $109.88
TRACTION BARS ONLY ....RACER'S NET $ 54.95
A FULL LINE OF SUPERCAR PREFORMANCE KITS COMING SOON!
ALL PRICES F.O.B. NEW YORK
NO C.O.D.'s, PLEASE
DEALER INQUIRIES INVITED

COMING SOON!
THE MOTION SUPERCAR CLUB

An exclusive club open ONLY to owners of supercars, regardless of make. Members will receive tuning tips, periodic bulletins on recommended factory and California speed goodies, special discounts, plus decals, membership cards and lots more.

COMING SOON!

HIGH-PERFORMANCE DEPT.
MOTION PERFORMANCE, INC.
598 SUNRISE HIGHWAY
BALDWIN, L.I., NEW YORK
516-223-3172-3178

CAR SALES
BALDWIN CHEVROLET
MERRICK RD. & CENTRAL AVE.
BALDWIN, L.I., NEW YORK
516-223-7700

his favorite carburetor, Edelbrock's 1015-cfm three-barrel Holley. Rosen had no regard for the power-robbing emissions controls hung on cars in the late sixties, so first thing that went in the trash was the A.I.R. (air injection pump) and all the plumbing. A set of Bill Thomas's headers was also bolted in place. Rosen also had a rear suspension kit that stiffened the rear leaves and virtually eliminated axle windup. Considering the work that went into the Phase 3 Baldwin-Motion 427 Camaro, the $4998.95 price tag was more than reasonable for a car guaranteed to turn the quarter in the mid 11s at 120 mph.

THE BALDWIN-MOTION PHASE III SS-427 CAMARO IS

SOMETHING ELSE!

It's not a **DRAG CAR**, but it's guaranteed to run 120 mph in 11.50 seconds or better

It's not a **SPORTS CAR**, but it'll out-handle any domestic production car including the Corvette

It's not a **FAMILY CAR**, but it holds four, has a trunk and is tractable enough for daily transportation

It must be **SOMETHING ELSE!**

FANTASTIC FIVE SS-427 prices start at $3,595.00

• SEND .50¢ for your copy of our '68½ Fantastic Five Chevrolet supercar & speed equipment racer's net catalog •

| THE BALDWIN-MOTION PERFORMANCE COMBINE: | BALDWIN CHEVROLET/Merrick Road & Central Avenue/Baldwin, L.I., N.Y./516-223-7700 |
| | MOTION PERFORMANCE, INC./High-Performance Sales-Service Division/598 Sunrise Highway/Baldwin, L.I.,N.Y./516-223-3172-3178 |

For 1968, Baldwin/Motion used a Corvette-style hood that appeared on 1967 Yenkos. Phase III Camaro was guaranteed to run the quarter mile in 11.5 seconds at 120 mph.

Motion could build a 1969 Camaro at any level of performance. They were blatant about their enthusiasm for street racing, and the articles that appeared in *Cars* always included a few street-racing pictures and teaser editorial.

Dana

Cruise down Long Beach Boulevard in South Gate, California, and you'd pass Dana Chevrolet. Co-owned by Shelby-American Guru Peyton Cramer, Dana Chevrolet advertised itself as the only high-performance dealer in California. As soon as the Camaro was released, Dana was dropping 427s in the cradle for locals.

The basic Dana conversion package consisted of a 425-horsepower 427 (the 1966 Corvette L72 usually) with single Holley four-barrel carburetor, SS trim package, heavy duty radiator, special heavy service springs and shocks, Goodyear F70 x 14 on six-inch wide wheels, and Dana/427 emblems.

Dana had one advantage that other Chevrolet high-performance dealers didn't, which was location. Being in Southern California, they caught the attention of the enthusiast magazines, resulting in numerous articles about Dana Chevrolet's 427 Camaro conversions. *Motor Trend* drove a 1967 Dana and noted "no matter how many 'hot' cars you've driven, the first time you really uncork a Dana Camaro you're bound to be awe-stricken if not outright panicked at the sheer magnitude of the forces unleashed."

Epilogue.

Whent the second generation Camaro hit the showrooms late in
February 1970, it signaled a new design philosophy, heavily
influenced by European sports cars. Much of the powertrain—except
the Z28's 302—was carried over and the basic structural engineering
configuration was retained. Visually, however, there were virtually no
vestiges of the first generation Camaro in the new.

Obviously, it was important to Chevrolet that the buying public
perceive this second generation car as a totally different Camaro. And
for the most part, the 1970's models were seen as all new, going so far
as to make the first generation look obsolete. That, of course, was the
essence of selling cars back then; next year's model was always up to
date: longer, lower and more desirable than its predecessors.

Looking back, the introduction of the second generation now pales
next to the success of the original Camaro. Sales of the first generation's
three-year run totaled a whisker shy of 700,000 units. It took the sec-
ond-generation six model years to equal that number. In fact, it wasn't
until the back-to-back-to-back success of the 1976—1978 model years
that the Camaro was able to equal the sales performance of the 1967
through 1969 models.

Today's collector prices also reflect this chasm between the first and
second generation. In the summer of 2001, a 1967 SS Coupe in number
one condition can command $20,000 while a 1967 or 1969 Z28 is
worth in excess of $38,000 and a 1968 SS396 coupe has traded hands
for more than $28,000. In contrast, a 1970 Z28 in perfect restored con-
dition trades for around $20,000 and an SS396 coupe sells for just
under $17,000. There's no reason to believe that gap in value will
change in the years to come.

Regardless of how it's measured, the first generation of Camaros
carved out an important niche in American automotive history.
Chevy's first pony car also made a strong statement for the resources
and talent within General Motors in the mid-Sixties. Created as a chal-
lenger to the wildly successful Mustang, the 1967 through 1969 model
soon became a mainstay within the Chevrolet lineup, and it will continue to be a favorite in the hearts of Bow Tie lovers for decades to
come.

art credits

GM Media Archives copyright 2001 General Motors Corporation:

Chapter 1, Pages: 2, 5, 6 (all), 8 (top), 10 (bottom)
Chapter 2, Pages: 14, 16, 25 (both), 26 (both), 28 (both),
29 (top), 37 (top), 44, 45
Chapter 3, Pages: 52, 53, 54 (top), 59
Chapter 4, pages: 70, 74 (both), 76 (both), 77 (both), 78
(all), 79 (both), 80, 81 (both), 82 (top)
Chapter 5, pages: 99 (both), 103 (top), 104, 117, 124, 131
(top)

Campbell-Ewald Advertising Agency of Record (GM advertising):

Chapter 3, Pages: 66, 68
Chapter 4, pages: 72, 96
Color Well, page: 2, 3
Chapter 5, page: 139

FORD:

Chapter 1, Pages: 7, 8 (bottom), 9, 10 (top), 11

Paul Zazarine

Chapter 2, Pages: 24, 34, 48

Car Life Magazine

Chapter 2, Pages: 41
Chapter 5, page: 138

Motor Trend Magazine

Chapter 2, Pages: 42

IMS

Chapter 2, Pages: 49, 50
Chapter 4, page: 93

Phil Kunz

Chapter 2, Page: 50
Chapter 4, page: 93

Bill Erdman

Chapter 3, Pages 55 (top), 58, 62 (bottom)

Holder Communications

Chapter 4, page: 82 (bottom)

John Corollo

Color Well, page: 6 (bottom)
Chapter 5, page: 113

Walt Thurn

Chapter 5, pages: 114, 120 (both)

Gold Dust Classics

Chapter 4, page: 91
Chapter 6, page: 152

Tom Shaw

Chapter 5, pages: 133, 135

Nickey

Chapter 6, page: 155

Baldwin/Motion

Chapter 6, pages: 156, 157, 158

From the collection of Paul Zazarine

Chapter 2, Pages: 17, 18, 19, 20, 21 (both), 23, 27, 29 (bottom), 31, 33, 35, 37 (bottom), 38, 39, 40 (both), 47 (both)

Chapter 3, Pages:54 (bottom), 55 (bottom), 57 (both), 60, 61, 62 (top), 63, 65 (both)

Chapter 4, pages: 83, 84, 85 (both), 87, 88, 89, 91 (bottom), 94 (both), 95 (both)

Color Well, page: 1 (both), 4 (both), 5 (both), 6 (top), 7 (both), 8 (both)

Chapter 5, pages: 98, 100 (both), 101, 102, 103 (bottom), 105 (all), 106 (both), 107, 108 (both), 109 (both), 110, 111, 115, 116, 118, 122, 125 (all), 126 (both), 127, 130, 131 (bottom), 134, 136, 137

Chapter 6, pages: 142, 145, 146, 147 (both), 148 (both), 149 (both), 150 (both), 151

In production of this book every effort was made to locate and obtain permission from the original artists of the included artwork.

acknowledgments

Part of the pleasure in writing about history is talking to those who were responsible for making it. In the course of researching this book, I had the privilege to speak with some of the people involved in creating and building the first-generation Camaro. Many had to reach quite a way back to recall incidents and events, and that's understandable. Can you remember what you were doing at work on June 3, 1966?

My thanks to:

Bill Erdman
Jim Ferron
Ford Photo Media Archives
GM Media Archives
Dave Holls
Tom Hoxie
Louie Ironside
Chuck Jordon
Paul King
Ralph Kramer

Phil Kunz
Mike Lamm
Alex Mair
Jim McFarland
Dave McLellan
Don McPherson
Tom Shaw
John W. Thawley III
Walt Thurn
Jack Underwood
Paul Van Valkenburg

about the author

Paul Zazarine is an award-winning author of 10 automotive books including *GTO Restoration Guide*, *How To Restore Your Musclecar* and *Glory Days*. He began his career in 1978 writing for club newsletters and freelancing for enthusiast magazines. He was the editor of Dobbs Publications' *Musclecar Review* from 1985–1988 and continued as a regular contributor and columnist for the magazine until 2000.

Zazarine was editor of *CorvetteFever* magazine from 1988 until 1995 and also served on the Board of Directors of the National Corvette Museum from 1990 to 1995, actively participating in the building of the museum. He also edited the NCM's newsletter from 1991–1994 and assisted with the museum's interior design and exhibit concepts.

An avid Corvette and musclecar enthusiast, Zazarine lives in Orlando, Florida.

index

T

The Camaro, 45
The Nation, 11
Thomas, Bill, 154, 157
Thompson, Mickey, 114
Titus, Jerry, 110-111, 119
Tulius, Bob, 99
Tuner, Curtis, 114
Turbo-Thrift 230 engine, 32

U

Unsafe at Any Speed, 11, 55
Unser, Al, 114

V

Van Valkenburg, Paul, 62, 104, 112-113
Variety, 45
Venke, Arlen, 153

W

W block engines, 31
Wenzel, Ben, 32, 63
Wintersteen, George, 111

Y

Yenko, Don, *see* Super Yenko Camero
Yunick, Smokey, 114

Z

Z/28 cars, 73, 98-141
  Boss (302) compared, 130, 132-136
  changes in package, 115, 128-129
  engine in, 100-102, 115, 120-123
  Heavy-Duty Service Package, 119, 124, 131
  1967 model, 99-113
  1968 model, 115-119
  1969 model, 121-141
  options packages for, 101, 102, 104-107, 118, 123, 124, 127, 128-129
  performance of, 112, 122, 136
  production of, 107, 115, 117, 121
  1967 racing season, 107-114
  1968 racing season, 115-119, 120, 121
  1969 racing season, 126-127, 130, 132, 137-141
  sales, 131, 133
ZL1 (427) engine, 142, 144-146, 152-154

Selected Books and Electronic Editions From Bentley Publishers

Audi

Audi TT Official Factory Repair Manual MY 2000 Electronic Edition CD-ROM
Audi of America ISBN 0-8376-0758-2

Audi A4/S4 Official Factory Repair Manual 1996-2000 Electronic Edition CD-ROM
Bentley Publishers ISBN 0-8376-0761-2

Audi 100, A6 Official Factory Repair Manual: 1992–1997, including S4, S6, Quattro and Wagon models
Audi of America ISBN 0-8376-0374-9

BMW

BMW 3 Series Enthusiast's Companion™
Jeremy Walton ISBN 0-8376-0220-3

BMW 6 Series Enthusiast's Companion™
Jeremy Walton ISBN 0-8376-0149-5

The BMW Enthusiast's Companion
BMW Car Club of America
ISBN 0-8376-0321-8

Unbeatable BMW: Eighty Years of Engineering and Motorsport Success
Jeremy Walton ISBN 0-8376-0206-8

Complete Roundel 1969-1998
8 CD-ROM set: 30 Years of the Magazine of the BMW Car Club of America, Inc.
BMW Car Club of America ISBN 0-8376-0322-6

BMW 3-Series (E46) Service Manual: 1999–2001, 323i, 325i, 325xi, 328i, 330i, 330xi Sedan, Coupe, Convertible, Sport Wagon
Bentley Publishers ISBN 0-8376-0320-X

BMW 3 Series (E36) Service Manual: 1992-1998, 318is/iC, 323is/iC, 325i/is/iC, 328i/is/iC, M3 *Bentley Publishers*
ISBN 0-8376-0326-9

BMW 3 Series (E30) Service Manual: 1984–1990 318i, 325, 325e(es), 325i(is), and 325i Convertible *Robert Bentley*
ISBN 0-8376-0325-0

BMW 5 Series (E34) Service Manual: 1989–1995 525i, 530i, 535i, 540i, including Touring *Bentley Publishers*
ISBN 0-8376-0319-6

BMW 7 Series (E32) Service Manual: 1988–1994, 735i, 735iL, 740i, 740iL, 750iL
Bentley Publishers ISBN 0-8376-0328-5

Chevrolet

Camaro Exposed 1967-1969: Designs, Decisions, and the Inside View
Paul Zazarine ISBN 0-8376-0876-7

Corvette Fuel Injection and Electronic Engine Management *Charles O. Probst, SAE*
ISBN 0-8376-0861-9

Corvette 427: Practical Restoration of a '67 Roadster *Don Sherman* ISBN 0-8376-0218-1

Chevrolet by the Numbers 1955-1959: The Essential Chevrolet Parts Reference
Alan Colvin ISBN 0-8376-0875-9

Chevrolet by the Numbers 1960-1964: The Essential Chevrolet Parts Reference
Alan Colvin ISBN 0-8376-0936-4

Chevrolet by the Numbers 1965-1969: The Essential Chevrolet Parts Reference
Alan Colvin ISBN 0-8376-0956-9

Chevrolet by the Numbers 1970-1975: The Essential Chevrolet Parts Reference
Alan Colvin ISBN 0-8376-0927-5

Chevrolet and GMC Light Truck Owner's Bible™ *Moses Ludel* ISBN 0-8376-0157-6

Ford

Ford F-Series Pickup Owner's Bible™
Moses Ludel ISBN 0-8376-0152-5

Ford Fuel Injection and Electronic Engine Control: 1988–1993 *Charles O. Probst, SAE*
ISBN 0-8376-0301-3

Ford Fuel Injection and Electronic Engine Control: 1980–1987 *Charles O. Probst, SAE*
ISBN 0-8376-0302-1

The Official Ford Mustang 5.0 Technical Reference & Performance Handbook 1979-1993 *Al Kirschenbaum*
ISBN 0-8376-0210-6

Porsche

Porsche 911 SC Service Manual 1978–1983
Bentley Publishers ISBN 0-8376-0290-4

Porsche 911 Carrera Service Manual 1984–1989
Bentley Publishers ISBN 0-8376-0291-2

Volkswagen

Battle for the Beetle: The Story of the Battle for the Giant VW Factory and the Car that Became an Icon Around the Globe
Karl Ludvigsen ISBN 08376-0071-5

Volkswagen Sport Tuning for Street and Competition *Per Schroeder*
ISBN 0-8376-0161-4

Volkswagen Scan Tool Companion: 1990-1995 Working with On-Board Diagnostics (OBD) Data for Engine Management Systems *Bentley Publishers*
ISBN 0-8376-0393-5

Volkswagen Model Documentation
Joachim Kuch ISBN 0-8376-0078-2

Volkswagen Jetta, Golf, GTI Service Manual: 1999-2002 Including 2.0L gasoline, 1.9L TDI, 2.8L VR6, and 1.8L turbo
Bentley Publishers ISBN 0-8376-0388-9

Volkswagen Passat Official Factory Repair Manual 1998-2000 Electronic Edition CD-ROM *Bentley Publishers* ISBN 0-8376-0763-9

Volkswagen New Beetle Official Factory Repair Manual 1998-2000 Electronic Edition CD-ROM *Bentley Publishers*
ISBN 0-8376-0760-4

Volkswagen New Beetle Service Manual: 1998-1999 2.0L Gasoline, 1.9L TDI Diesel, 1.8L Turbo *Bentley Publishers*
ISBN 0-8376-0385-4

Volkswagen Jetta, Golf, GTI, Cabrio Service Manual: 1993–1999, including Jetta$_{III}$ and Golf$_{III}$ *Robert Bentley*
ISBN 0-8376-0366-8

Volkswagen GTI, Golf, Jetta Service Manual 1985-1992 Electronic Edition CD-ROM
Bentley Publishers ISBN 0-8376-0759-0

Super Beetle, Beetle and Karmann Ghia Official Service Manual Type 1: 1970–1979
Volkswagen United States ISBN 0-8376-0096-0

Driving

The Unfair Advantage *Mark Donohue*
ISBN 0-8376-0073-1 (hardcover)
0-8376-0069-3 (paperback)

A French Kiss With Death: Steve McQueen and the Making of Le Mans
Michael Keyser ISBN 0-8376-0234-3

Going Faster! Mastering the Art of Race Driving *The Skip Barber Racing School*
ISBN 0-8376-0227-0

The Racing Driver *Denis Jenkinson*
ISBN 0-8376-0201-7

The Speed Merchants: A Journey Through the World of Motor Racing 1969-1972
Michael Keyser ISBN 0-8376-0232-7

Sports Car and Competition Driving
Paul Frère with foreword *by Phil Hill*
ISBN 0-8376-0202-5

Think To Win: The New Approach to Fast Driving *Don Alexander with foreword by Mark Martin* ISBN 0-8376-0070-7

Driving Forces: The Grand Prix Racing World Caught in the Maelstrom of the Third Reich *Peter Stevenson*
ISBN 0-8376-0217-3

Engineering

Supercharged! Design, Testing, and Installation of Supercharger Systems
Corky Bell ISBN 0-8376-0168-1

Bosch Fuel Injection and Engine Management *Charles O. Probst, SAE*
ISBN 0-8376-0300-5

Maximum Boost: Designing, Testing, and Installing Turbocharger Systems
Corky Bell ISBN 0-8376-0160-6

Race Car Aerodynamics *Joseph Katz*
ISBN 0-8376-0142-8

Other Enthusiast Titles

Road & Track Illustrated Automotive Dictionary *John Dinkel* ISBN 0-8376-0143-6

Harley-Davidson Evolution V-Twin Owner's Bible™ *Moses Ludel*
ISBN 0-8376-0146-0

Jeep Owner's Bible™ *Moses Ludel*
ISBN 0-8376-0154-1